CONGRATULATIONS!
Johns Hopkins Carey Business School
The Edward St. John Department of Real Estate
Master of Science in Real Estate
Class of 2008 - 2009

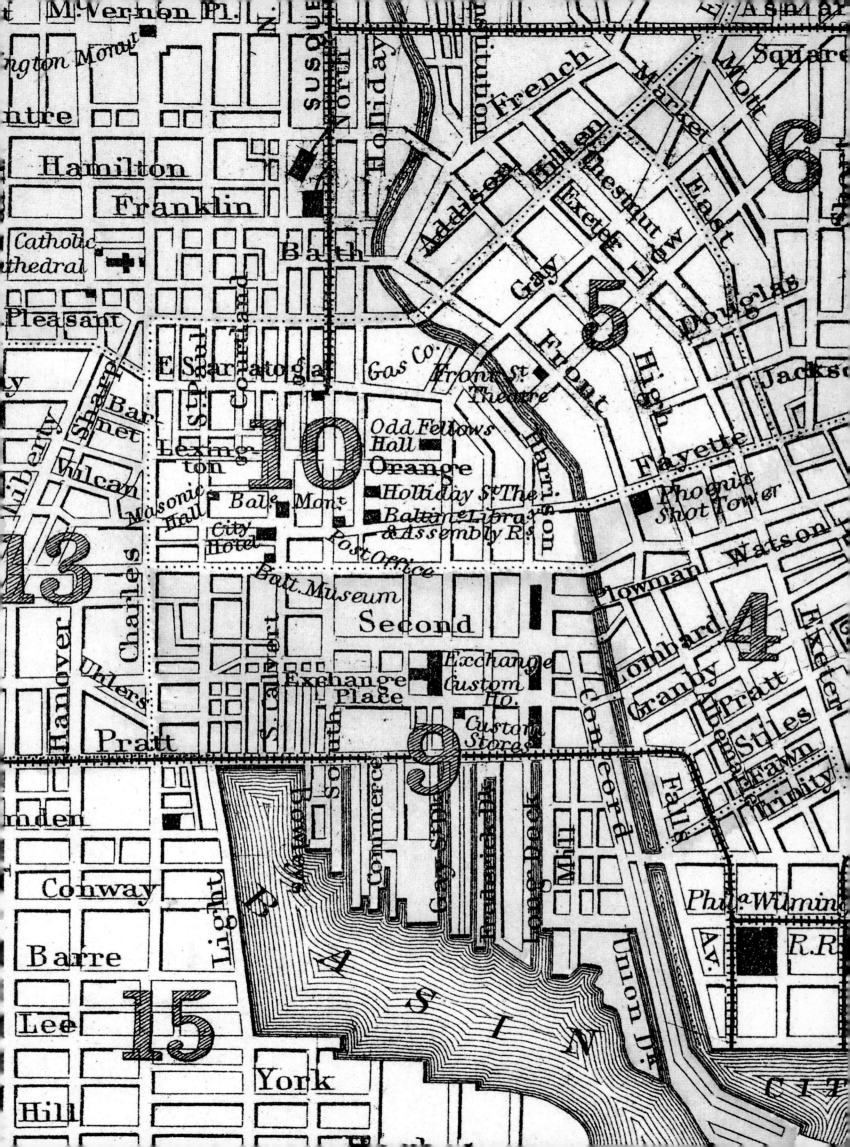

THE LIVING CITY

THE LIVING CITY

BALTIMORE'S CHARLES CENTER & INNER HARBOR DEVELOPMENT

Photographs by Marion E. Warren

Text by Michael P. McCarthy

Foreword by Walter Sondheim, Jr.

MHS

MARYLAND HISTORICAL SOCIETY

BALTIMORE

$\mathcal{M}d\mathcal{H}_S$

The Maryland Historical Society extends special thanks to
Allfirst Bank for its generous support of this publication.

Library of Congress Cataloging-in-Publication Data

Warren, Marion E.
  The living city : Baltimore's Charles Center and Inner Harbor development /
photographs by Marion E. Warren ; text by Michael P. McCarthy.
    p. cm.
  Includes bibliographical references (p.) and index.
  ISBN 0-938420-68-2
    1. Urban renewal—Maryland—Baltimore—History. 2. City
planning—Maryland—Baltimore—History. 3. Charles Center (Baltimore, Md.) 4. Inner
Harbor (Baltimore, Md.) 5. Baltimore (Md.)—Buildings, structures, etc. I. McCarthy,
Michael P. II. Title

HT177.B35 W37 2001
307.3'416'097526—dc21

                                                                        99-049601

The paper used in this publication meets the minimum requirements
of the American National Standard for Information Sciences Permanence of Paper
for Printed Library Materials ANSI Z39.48-1984

Photographs

Cover: Baltimore from the Inner Harbor in the early 1980s

Front endpaper & facing page: Detail from S. Augustus Mitchell Jr., Plan of Baltimore, *1860*

Pages 2 & 3: Aerial photograph of Baltimore taken circa 1960

Pages 6 & 7: Aerial photograph of downtown Baltimore circa 1958

Page 8: Charles Center in 1964

Closing endpaper & facing page: Baltimore looking north across the Inner Harbor, 1988

Contents

XII   THE LIVING CITY

Foreword

Those who were involved in the first twenty-five years or so of Baltimore's downtown renaissance are frequently asked, "How in the world did it come about? What did the place look like before all this happened?" This book supplies answers to those questions. We made plenty of mistakes during those days, but it is fair to consider dispassionately what the city would be like if it had not engaged in the extensive effort to rebuild a substantial area of its downtown. This was an undertaking that generated a genuine partnership of the municipal government and the business and neighborhood communities.

Imagine what the city would be like today if the downtown rejuvenation had not taken place. Certainly the persistent problems with our tax base would be greatly multiplied. Our significant tourist and convention industries are of very recent vintage. Indeed, some of us remember when Baltimore was known chiefly as an obstruction to through traffic on the pre-interstate route between Washington and Philadelphia or New York. (Not so many years ago, if I had seen a tour bus on Pratt Street I would have been certain that the driver had taken a wrong turn and become lost on a journey to some other city! Today the city has trouble finding parking areas for the steady arrival of such vehicles.)

It is a real error to subscribe to the populist notion that the financial resources utilized for the inner-city renewal represented a deprivation of attention to urgent neighborhood needs. Some of the funding of Charles Center and the Inner Harbor was not legally available for other uses. More importantly, an examination of all the public resources available during the period of intensive development revealed that eighty-five percent were used in the neighborhood programs, and only fifteen percent were spent in the downtown efforts. (Most of what is done in the Inner Harbor, for example, is more dramatically visible than activities involving residential areas; however, the latter may often be of greater import and value to the people involved.)

Despite all the bumps and potholes, Baltimore keeps on a course of revitalization that began half a century ago. Today the computer serves a valuable purpose as a communications tool. So do many other new technologies. But there is something special about face-to-face contacts and mingling with crowds enjoying the sights. This is why downtowns will always play an important role in the life of cities. This wonderfully valuable and entertaining book chronicles in picture and word what happened to transform us and set us on that upward journey.

Walter Sondheim Jr.

Preface & Acknowledgments

Marion Warren is best known for his images of farmers, fishermen, and the small towns of Maryland that we see in *Bringing Back the Bay* (1994), a book on the Chesapeake that he did with his daughter Mame. But he also has an eye for the lives and landscape of larger communities. Several years ago, I went to see some of his Baltimore photographs in the Maryland State Archives in Annapolis. I happened to meet Mame, who at the time was curator of photographs. "You should use those wonderful photographs for another book," I said. Whereupon Mame all but grabbed my jacket lapels in her enthusiasm. "Give my father a call," she said, handing me his phone number. It seems Marion had the same idea that I did, but Mame was unable to help out on the writing side because she was involved in a project of her own. And so, instead of Warren and Warren, this one became a Warren and McCarthy book. With the exception of historic images, all photographs are Marion's, with most of them taken from the beginning of urban renewal in the late 1950s to the early 1980s, when Charles Center and the Inner Harbor were well underway.

In a sense, our book really started when Marion had a conversation with Charles Lamb back in the mid-1950s. At the time, Lamb was a principal of the fledgling architectural firm in Annapolis that would become RTKL. Marion was also an Annapolis resident, having settled there after World War II to start a business as a commercial photographer. Lamb had a couple of projects that needed photographing and asked if Marion be interested. He was indeed, Marion replied, but he had scant experience in architectural photography. Lamb was confident it would work out, and Marion proved him right. The Greater Baltimore Committee was soon asking Marion to document downtown on the eve of urban renewal. Once the work began, he was on assignment for others as well, including the Charles Center–Inner Harbor Development Office, the Rouse Company, and RTKL, which was to become a major design firm for both Charles Center and the Inner Harbor.

Marion's photographs show us the changes in downtown, as it shifted toward tourism, high technology, and finance. Like many other cities, Baltimore found itself losing business to the new suburban malls and industrial parks of the Automobile Age. Its shipping and manufacturing would also soon suffer from the effects of world competition. Charles Center and the Inner Harbor were projects to meet those challenges. To be sure, many problems remain, but the new downtown brings jobs and revenue to the entire community. My text provides the reader with a narrative of the story that Marion is telling in photographs. The publication of this book would not have been possible without the generous support of Allfirst, the parent bank of the former

First National Bank of Maryland. The gift reflects the commitment to downtown of Allfirst's chairman, Frank P. Bramble, and we are grateful for his help. We would also like to thank J. Michael Riley, Senior Vice President at Allfirst, who from the beginning shared our enthusiasm for the project.

The following shared their knowledge of downtown Baltimore: David W. Barton Jr., Barbara J. Bonnell, William Boucher III, Morton Hoffman, David W. Kornblatt, Martin Millspaugh, Garrett Power, Larry Reich, Archibald C. Rogers, Laurie Schwartz, Walter Sondheim Jr., and David A. Wallace. Many of the above played important roles in the Charles Center and Inner Harbor projects as planners, business leaders, and officials of public and private agencies. (Some wore more than one hat.) They helped me to get my facts straight and see the decision-making process from various perspectives. Several commented on early drafts, and Walter Sondheim even read two. Any remaining errors are mine.

Historians also rely on a wide range of other sources, from letters, memos, reports, and newspapers, to maps and photographs. As researchers, we hope enough documents make their way into archives and libraries for us to take another look at past events. I was fortunate to find plenty for this project in the Maryland Historical Society's library and the Maryland Room of the Enoch Pratt Free Library. I would also like to thank Rebecca Gumby at the Baltimore City Archives and Tom Hollowak at the Special Collections department of the University of Baltimore's Langsdale Library for their help in accessing those rich collections. Much of the secondary research was done at Langsdale Library. My thanks in particular to Steve LaBash, Carol Mason, Mary Schwartz, Tammy Taylor, and Susan Wheeler for all the book and periodical searches they cheerfully performed.

Marion and I would also like to thank the Press at the Maryland Historical Society and our editor, Donna B. Shear. I dedicate my efforts to my wife, Carol, who has shared my interest in cities for over three decades. Marion does the same for his wife, Mary, who has been looking at his photographs even longer.

Michael P. McCarthy
Baltimore, Maryland
December 2001

THE LIVING CITY

I.
Baltimore

From Decline to Renewal

In 1817, William Strickland, the artist and architect, made his well-known engraving of Baltimore as it looked in 1752. It is based on a sketch made by John Moale, a member of a prominent land-owning family, who climbed what is now Federal Hill for a perspective across the Inner Harbor. Two women fetch water from a spring near the southwest corner. Wading in the shallows nearby, four fishermen haul in a catch in their nets. The rest of the broad expanse of the Inner Harbor is empty except for two ships—a bay sloop and a more impressive brigantine, with its two masts and square rigging. Both ride quietly at anchor in the calm waters. Founded in 1729, Baltimore looks like a sleepy village, which it more or less still was in 1752, with only around two hundred inhabitants.[1] Real growth would start a few years later when the wheat of Baltimore's hinterland became an important commodity. The city got another boost during the American Revolution when other ports were occupied by the British. In the nineteenth century the Baltimore & Ohio Railroad made it a gateway to the West, and the city became a major manufacturing center as well as a port. Location had taken the little hamlet a long way.

Today the port is no longer what it used to be, in large part because of the significant shift in America's trade from Europe to the Pacific Rim. Baltimore was also once the main port for the Southeast; now it has stiff competition from Norfolk, Charleston, Savannah, and Jacksonville, because they are closer to the booming Sun Belt markets. In its heyday in the 1950s, Bethlehem Steel hired thirty thousand workers at its Sparrows Point plant; today it has about four thousand. The Pratt cannery on Key Highway reflects just how much the local economy has changed. Once one of dozens that processed bay oysters, as well as regional fruits and vegetables, the cannery is now home of the Baltimore Museum of Industry. An apt reminder of past glory, but not necessarily a melancholy one. Cities are always changing, and we can see a new Baltimore as we look around the Inner Harbor today.

Downtown Takes Shape

In the early years, downtown consisted of a few buildings at the water's edge. Here were the shippers and insurance agents, who handled the business of the port. Here also were the wholesalers and the handful of merchants in the retail trade. As shipping expanded, so did the need for more space at the waterfront. New streets were added from landfill (Lombard and Pratt) south of the original shoreline at Water Street. The business district began to move northward. Retail districts grew on Baltimore and Howard Streets, the latter having been the site of a farmer's market. Another was on Charles Street; it served the genteel Mount Vernon neighborhood a few blocks to the north. On the east side of downtown, bankers and insurers clustered in the blocks around Bal-

Facing page: Downtown about 1925. Bay steamers line the wharves at Light Street. (Baltimore Gas & Electric Company)

Above: William Strickland's view of Baltimore, based on a 1752 sketch by John Moale. Larger vessels called at nearby Fells Point, where the water was deeper. (Maryland Historical Society, Baltimore City Life Collections)

Right: A sketch of the northwest side of downtown as it appeared in 1812, by surveyor Thomas Poppleton. (Maryland Historical Society)

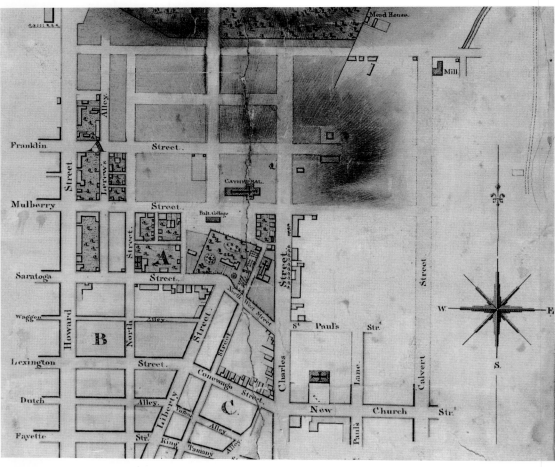

timore, Redwood, and Calvert Streets, in what would become the financial district. Nearby a civic district of sorts was beginning to take form, with city government buildings going up on Holliday and Fayette Streets.

The age of industry brought growth in population and spatial size as well. The streetcar was responsible for a good deal of the latter. Introduced in Baltimore in 1859, the new technology encouraged developers to build in neighborhoods like Bolton Hill and Charles Village. Later on the suburban frontier spread to more distant spots like Roland Park, Catonsville, and Pikesville as middle-class commuters and their families sought the greenery of the countryside. The streetcar also had its share of blue-collar riders. They went downtown occasionally for shopping and civic events, and some commuted on the streetcars to factory jobs, or to work at the distant shipyards and steel mills. Overall, however, streetcars had less of an impact on working-class residents be-

cause few could afford a suburban home; most lived near their places of employment in the industrial districts. These became distinct sub-communities with their own neighborhood shopping districts, like Light Street in South Baltimore and Eastern Avenue in Highlandtown. In many respects, downtown was the biggest beneficiary of the streetcar because all the lines headed in that direction. Retailing—and the department stores in particular—reaped the rewards of a central location. O'Neill's and the Hub were located on Charles Street; Hochschild-Kohn, Hecht's, Hutzler's, and Stewart's on the west side at Howard and Lexington, in what became the main retail district by the turn of the century.

Downtown also saw the growth of entertainment districts. East Baltimore Street served the nearby working-class residential neighborhoods. It offered music hall and family fare before becoming notorious as the "Block" of strip joints in later decades. On the west side, in the vicinity of Eutaw

The Inner Harbor in the early 1850s. Sailing ships of all kinds plied the Chesapeake Bay well into the twentieth century. (Enoch Pratt Free Library)

and Howard Streets, were most of the downtown venues for vaudeville acts and stage shows, as well as the movie theaters. They commingled with all the shops and stores that were also in the neighborhood. Manufacturing is not usually associated with downtown, but it flourished in the streetcar era, particularly in clothing, which was a major Baltimore industry. Some of this work took place on the periphery of downtown, in small sweatshops like those in the row houses of East Baltimore. Most companies were in downtown locations near the main retail and commercial districts. One of the biggest and best known was in the Paca-Pratt Building, which was the factory of Henry Sonneborn and Company from the turn of the century until the 1930s; several smaller companies continued to use some of the space after that. The short block of Hopkins Place (in midtown between Baltimore and Lombard Streets) was another center for clothing manufacturing. As late as 1956 the city directory listed six manufac-

turers on various floors in buildings along the street, among them Jos. A. Bank, the menswear company.

Wholesaling was another big business in the blocks of lower midtown. On Lombard, everything from shoes to printing supplies, on Pratt the fruit and vegetable wholesalers, and much the same on South Light Street. Tobacco warehouses were in the neighborhood, as were manufacturers like McCormick and Company, the spice firm on Light Street. It had been there since 1921, when it consolidated its local manufacturing facilities. The nine-story building had twelve and one-half acres of floor space. The whitewashed exterior made it a local landmark, and the smell of spices often wafted about the neighborhood.

The Dilemmas of the Auto Age

The streetcar era ended officially on November 6, 1963, when the No. 8 line, which passed through downtown on its way between Catonsville and Towson, made its last run. Unofficially, it had been over as early as 1946, the city having approved at that time the first major phasing out of streetcar lines for buses. Baltimoreans are nostalgic about streetcars, but back then they complained bitterly about the slow ride and unreliable service provided by the Baltimore Transit Company. Buses improved the speed, but service remained a headache. Given the choice, Baltimoreans preferred to drive their own cars if they had them, and increasingly many did. The federal government encouraged them with the Interstate Highway Act of 1956.

The automobile transformed Baltimore and the adjacent counties. Suburban Baltimore County's population jumped from 270,000 to 492,000 between 1950 and 1960, Anne Arundel's, from 117,400 to 206,600. Most of those newcomers were moving from Baltimore to fulfill the American Dream of owning a home in suburbia and raising their kids amidst lawns and greenery. (And for many ex-GIs, the government was helping them to do so, with low-cost federal mortgage programs.) Some were leaving for less lofty reasons. Baltimore was a southern city, which had its own Jim Crow laws until the Civil Rights era. To its credit, Baltimore began integrating its schools in 1954, the year of the Supreme Court's ruling in *Brown v. Board of Education*. But this only increased the suburban flow; between 1950 and 1960 Baltimore's white population dropped from 723,700 to 610,400. As whites moved out, blacks began moving into older white neighborhoods like Edmondson, which shifted dramatically in race between 1950 and 1960. Overall, black residential numbers increased —from 225,000 to 328,600—as a new generation of migrants from the South headed northward

Before the 1950s, black shoppers had been more or less limited to the stores along Pennsylvania Avenue, which was in the heart of black Baltimore on the west side. Now they provided new customers for the downtown department stores. Overall sales, however, were still down because whites were not shopping there as much as before. In part this was simply because suburban housewives—who were important customers—no

longer bothered with formal trips downtown; they preferred the proximity of the new malls and the casual shopping there. But racial prejudice was also a factor as more blacks shopped downtown, a development that had "unfortunate consequences," as a report on retail trade noted. "Retailers are not particularly equipped to solve national social problems. Yet to a large extent, the future of Downtown's retailing depends upon this."[2]

In the fall of 1954, O'Neill's, long a landmark on Charles Street, was the first of the department stores to close its doors. So did many of midtown's smaller retail stores, who were especially hard hit by the competition of the malls. On Lexington between Charles and Liberty Streets, property assessments were nearly double actual commercial real estate values. Turnover of businesses in prime locations on Charles and Howard, as well as on Baltimore and Lexington, was increasing in figures of "alarming proportions" according to one local real estate expert, who saw little hope for reversing the trend. As for office space, the situation was not much brighter. To be sure, relatively few private firms had yet left for the suburbs. But federal agencies were on the move, in

O'Neill's department store at the corner of Lexington and Charles Streets. This would become the site for One Charles Center, the first building in the urban renewal project. (1960)

Ships carrying produce and other bulk items used the city piers on Pratt Street into the 1950s. The piles of lumber are on Pier Six. (1955)

Left: Obsolete wharves and terminal buildings along Light Street (upper middle) had been cleared by 1950, but Bethlehem Steel Dry Dock (left) and city piers (right) were still handling ships. (1960)

Above: The Bromo Seltzer Tower (now the Baltimore Arts Tower). A revolving steel replica of the Bromo Seltzer bottle atop the building was removed in 1936 when it became structurally unsound. (c.1960)

Above: Howard Street near Fayette Street looking north. This was Baltimore's main shopping district, with four department stores nearby. One was Stewart's, on the right. (1950)

Right: A block on West Baltimore Street that would soon give way to urban renewal. The cast-iron facade dates from the nineteenth century. (1971)

part to stop leasing and also because of decentralizing policies at the time when the threat of atomic attack was real. The Social Security Administration shifted thousands of its employees to new buildings at Woodlawn on the beltway in Baltimore County, leaving vacant approximately 600,000 square feet in twelve different buildings.

Parking was another headache for downtown. The city tried to help with an Off-Street Parking Commission (1949), one of the first of its kind in the country. It provided loans to private operators to buy properties and build garages and parking lots. By 1953 sixteen were open, and another two under construction. They added 3,300 spaces to provide a total of 4,900 downtown. But the extra parking could not keep up with the inexorable demands of the auto age. (In 1998 the city had about 24,000 spaces and needed 3,000 more.) Many of the new facilities were not convenient. The Lexington Market garage, for example, had 1,325 spaces, but this proved to be a bit too far from the west side department stores that it was intended to serve. Hutzler's was the only department store with a garage, a small one added in the 1920s. The others were reluctant because of the great cost for land acquisition and construction. By the 1950s sales had sagged at all the stores, including Hutzler's. By contrast, in the suburbs where malls came equipped with generous parking, the branches of the downtown stores boomed. Between 1947 and 1957, they added more than 700,000 feet of new space, and sales doubled there.

The Planning Begins

What could the city do? Pittsburgh caught Baltimore's attention because of its success in turning an abandoned industrial district between the Monongahela and Susquehanna Rivers in downtown Pittsburgh into a "Golden Triangle" that included Gateway Center, a complex of new offices and landscaped plazas. A private-public partnership called the Allegheny Conference on Community Development was in charge of the project. At the time federal Title I urban renewal programs did not fund projects for business districts, and Richard K. Mellon,

of the Mellon bank family, played a vital role in assuring financial support. Baltimore had no one with Mellon's financial clout, but civic leaders felt that if an aging industrial city like Pittsburgh was turning itself around, so could Charm City.

In 1955 a group of the city's leading businessmen organized the Greater Baltimore Committee. Like the Allegheny Conference on Community Development, the name reflected a regional focus and awareness of the centrifugal forces affecting the downtown area. The GBC included businessmen who had organized the Committee for Downtown a year earlier. The membership of the business associations overlapped to a great extent, and the GBC became the umbrella organization for the downtown effort. James W. Rouse headed the Greater Baltimore Committee's first urban renewal committee.

Rouse might seem a surprising choice to head a downtown urban renewal committee because most of his own projects were in the suburbs. He had built malls at Harundale near Glen Burnie and Mondawmin in northwest Baltimore in the 1950s. Rouse had

Howard Street looking north. The Hochschild-Kohn department store is on the left; next to it is Hutzler Brothers. (1952)

Facing page: The Central Business District before renewal. Liberty Street (crossing on lower left) marked the western boundary of the Charles Center project. (1958)

Gas station on Pratt Street. (1961)

also turned a golf course in North Baltimore into the townhouse community of Cross Keys. It had some shops and offices, an apartment building, and even a hotel. It was something of a prototype for what Rouse would do later at Columbia, his new city between Baltimore and Washington. But Rouse was also deeply concerned about the quality of life for the less affluent in the inner city. In his view, a healthy central business district was necessary for generating jobs and the tax revenues that would strengthen the entire community. Rouse was an active member of Baltimore's Citizens Planning and Housing Association and promoted its goals of home ownership and community-based, self-help programs in older neighborhoods.[3] The first report of Rouse's GBC urban renewal committee said

the inner city should once again become "a community of healthy neighborhoods where people can be proud and happy to live and raise families." The key to successful renewal was putting land—"the city's most precious resource"— back to work helping everyone. Baltimore needed to do so "with bolder planning, better organization and a much faster pace."[4]

In 1956, with money raised from members, the GBC created a planning council to assist Baltimore's city government in developing a first project as well as a long-term master plan for the renewal of downtown. Here again, the GBC had looked to the example of the Allegheny Conference. The Pittsburgh organization had a similar planning council, which oversaw its "Golden Triangle" project. Hunter Moss was appointed the

A newsboy sells papers at Fayette and Park Streets. The view is to the east. (1962)

chairman. He was a highly respected commercial real estate consultant who had worked with Rouse in earlier years in mortgage banking. Moss led a national search for a director of planning and hired David A. Wallace. Wallace came from Philadelphia where he had worked with Edmund Bacon as director of planning for the Philadelphia Redevelopment Authority, an agency that was responsible for that city's Penn Center project. Wallace was a licensed architect then in his early forties. He also had a doctorate from Harvard in city planning and had worked as a supervising planner for the Chicago Housing Authority before taking the Philadelphia job. Wallace put together a talented staff that included George E. Kostritsky, an architect with a master's degree in planning from the Massachusetts

Institute of Technology; Harry B. Cooper, a planner and economist from New York; and William H. Potts Jr., a landscape architect who had been a planner for the Philadelphia Redevelopment Authority.

In 1955 Archibald C. Rogers had taken a year's leave from his architecture practice to serve as the first executive director of the Greater Baltimore Committee. His remarks at a Kiwanis meeting in August summed up the quandary facing the planners. If suburban flight has become a reality, he asked, which must be worked with rather than resisted, what should we do about downtown?

Should we try to attract people back into the core to support the retail businesses that have flourished in the past? Or should we

Left: Looking west on Baltimore Street at Hanover Street toward the present site of the Mercantile–Safe Deposit & Trust Building. (c.1962)

Below: The east side of Baltimore Street. The Lord Baltimore Hotel rises above the block on the right. (c.1962)

Facing page: Looking east on Baltimore Street, the Maryland National Bank Building is visible center, left; it is now the Bank of America Building. The Tower Building, center right, was torn down in 1986. (c.1962)

Looking south on Park Avenue at the corner of Fayette Street. A streetcar arrives at left. (1962)

make of the core a kind of "world's fair"— gay and charming, something aesthetically pleasing, a place where all would want to come and trade and work—a bazaar, a fair, an urban park?—that serves as the heart for the entire metropolitan area? Perhaps this should be the objective and perhaps not. It is too early to say. Nevertheless, one thing I think is obvious: to do anything with the heart of our city we must all become 24-hour citizens of Baltimore and that, to me, seems the most important step of all. For if we all are 24-hour citizens then we will no longer ignore the problems that beset us here in the heart of our metropolitan area.[5]

The planners realized that downtown revitalization had to be selective. Some traditional functions, such as light manufacturing and wholesaling activities, could no longer be supported since suburban locations had become more attractive. The future of retailing was not as bleak, but it appeared that the downtown was going to have to accept a permanently lower market share. The goal, as they saw it, was to bolster downtown's role as an office center.

Class-A office buildings already enjoyed a ninety-nine percent occupancy rate. This impressive figure was largely a result of the lack of new construction during the Great Depression and World War II. It was widely felt that Baltimore badly needed more modern office space in order to stay competitive. Good news came, however, from a survey of business leaders. Overall they had a positive view toward downtown. They liked the greater availability of clerical staff and easy commuting, and the personal interactions of downtown, like schmoozing with a business associate over lunch at popular spots like Miller Brothers restaurant on Fayette Street.

The GBC planning council was also encouraged by a project of the Commercial Credit Company. In 1957 it opened the first new office building in downtown Baltimore since the 1920s. The company had consolidated operations (one thousand employees at eight offices around the city) at the new building, which was located at the north end of the financial district, above Saratoga Street at 300 St. Paul Place. The new headquarters was twice the size of the company's immediate needs, so the extra space was being leased. Despite premium rentals, it went in a few months to major companies like Western Maryland Railway, Chesapeake & Potomac Telephone, Bethlehem Steel, and Alcoa. Alexander E. Duncan, the founder and chairman of Commercial Credit, admitted that some of his closest friends had advised him against a big building in Baltimore, but results turned out just fine.

And so the planning council decided on an office complex with a hotel, theater and some retail space. The project would have other attractions, including ample parking. In their proposal the planners recognized that the automobile was now "a major factor on the urban scene." They also said the most efficient parking "must be within a block of the driver's destination." Cars would be put in underground garages in the center. This would make them accessible and also allow a better use of the land in and around the project.

Choosing a Site

In the summer of 1956, a year before the planning council was underway, Arthur D. McVoy, the head of the city's planning department, proposed a new master plan for downtown. McVoy had his doubts about major capital investment in midtown, particularly in retail stores, given their declining sales. Instead he recommended more parking and pedestrian malls as a way of attracting suburbanites back to the existing retail district. As part of McVoy's plan, the financial district, which was several blocks north of the harbor around Calvert and Baltimore Streets, would be extended southward, back to its historic roots nearer the waterfront. McVoy also recommended a similar southward extension of the city's government center, along a mall that would provide a visual link between the City Hall area and the Inner Harbor.

In McVoy's view the Inner Harbor was ripe for renewal because it was no longer doing much business as a port operation. Bay steamers, as well as the boats that carried seafood and produce, had become casualties of the auto age. A few small freighters

The old Sun *Building at Charles between Baltimore and Redwood Streets. This would become the site for the Morris A. Mechanic Theater. (1964)*

called at the municipal piers on the north side, but shipping was shifting down the harbor to deep-water facilities such as those in Dundalk, which could handle a new generation of bigger ships. McVoy noted that cities like Stockholm, Rio de Janeiro, Venice, and Copenhagen had taken advantage of their "water-oriented" settings.[6]

The GBC liked McVoy's approach and backed the Inner Harbor as the location for the Civic Center (now Arena), a multi-purpose facility that the city was planning to build. The business group hired the prominent architect Pietro Belluschi as a consultant. He recommended a soaring pavilion at the corner of Light and Pratt Streets where Harborplace stands today. The proposal had the support of many groups, including the Maryland Port Authority and the Steamship Trade Association of Baltimore, which both recognized that the Inner Harbor's shipping days were over. The commission in charge of making a choice, however, eventually said no in 1957, largely on cost concerns.

David Wallace had followed all these developments with great interest. He had recently arrived in Baltimore, and did not play any role in the decision on the Civic Center's Inner Harbor location. However, he

Redwood Street and Hopkins Place looking east. At one time this was a busy wholesale and light manufacturing district. (1962)

Facing page: The Charles Center planners prepared an elaborate report to promote the project. This is a land-use map of downtown. (Charles Center, 1958)

did prepare a report for the GBC in February 1957 on Belluschi's proposal. Wallace shared the commission's concerns, which included the theoretical threat of flooding at a waterfront site, but he supported the site because of the "all-important long-range objectives." He also felt the Inner Harbor location offered a "rare opportunity to make the Civic Center the beginning of a renewal chain reaction rather than an end in itself."[7]

When the planning council staff set out to identify a site for its own project, it reviewed McVoy's plan. The staff was impressed with "the strong pull of the harbor" in his approach, and it also agreed that "the harbor is a natural for park development around which would be created very desirable building sites, commercial as well as residential." They concluded, however, that "Perhaps one has to forget the existence of the Inner Harbor as an element of influence in the plan for downtown (pretend it doesn't exist)."[8] This seems to be an extraordinary statement for planners to make, as it implies that they should ignore an obvious focal point. But reviving the existing office and shopping district was the GBC's priority, and it was understandable

to doubt that an Inner Harbor project would have an impact that far north. The staff was particularly concerned with assisting the Howard and Lexington area, which faced the prospect, they felt, of becoming "a skid row," if it did not get some help.

And so the planning council decided to look elsewhere. It considered several sites, including the Mercy Hospital area to the north and the University of Maryland to the west. The final choice was a midtown area bounded by Saratoga on the north, Liberty on the west, Charles on the east, and Lombard on the south. It was a declining district that had a mixture of retailing, wholesaling, and light manufacturing. The planners called it an "economic valley" that offered an ideal place for new investment, in large part because it lay directly between the city's retail and financial districts. Wallace later said, "The opportunity jumped at us after we began to get an understanding of how the central business district really worked."[9]

In the early days the planning council referred to the endeavor simply as Project One. Once the site was selected, suggestions for a permanent name included Key Central, Park Center, and Liberty Center. Hunter Moss liked Liberty Center, but council member W. Arthur Grotz, president of the Western Maryland Railway, felt the word "had lost its positive connotations by misuse." He suggested that the project take the name of another, less ideological boundary street. And so it became Charles Center.[10]

The GBC did an artful job of selling the project. It got help from the Barton-Gillet advertising agency, with David A. Barton Jr., coordinating the campaign. Perhaps most impressive was the design of the planning council's report that presented the Charles Center proposal: oversized in format, with bold graphics and foldout pages. (*Fortune* magazine called it the best of its kind that year.) Barton felt the big size was important to capture attention. The size had another purpose; at fourteen inches square, the report was too big to fit inside a filing cabinet and would likely remain on a desk where it might have a better chance of getting read. The Charles Center report was similar to one published in 1909 by another

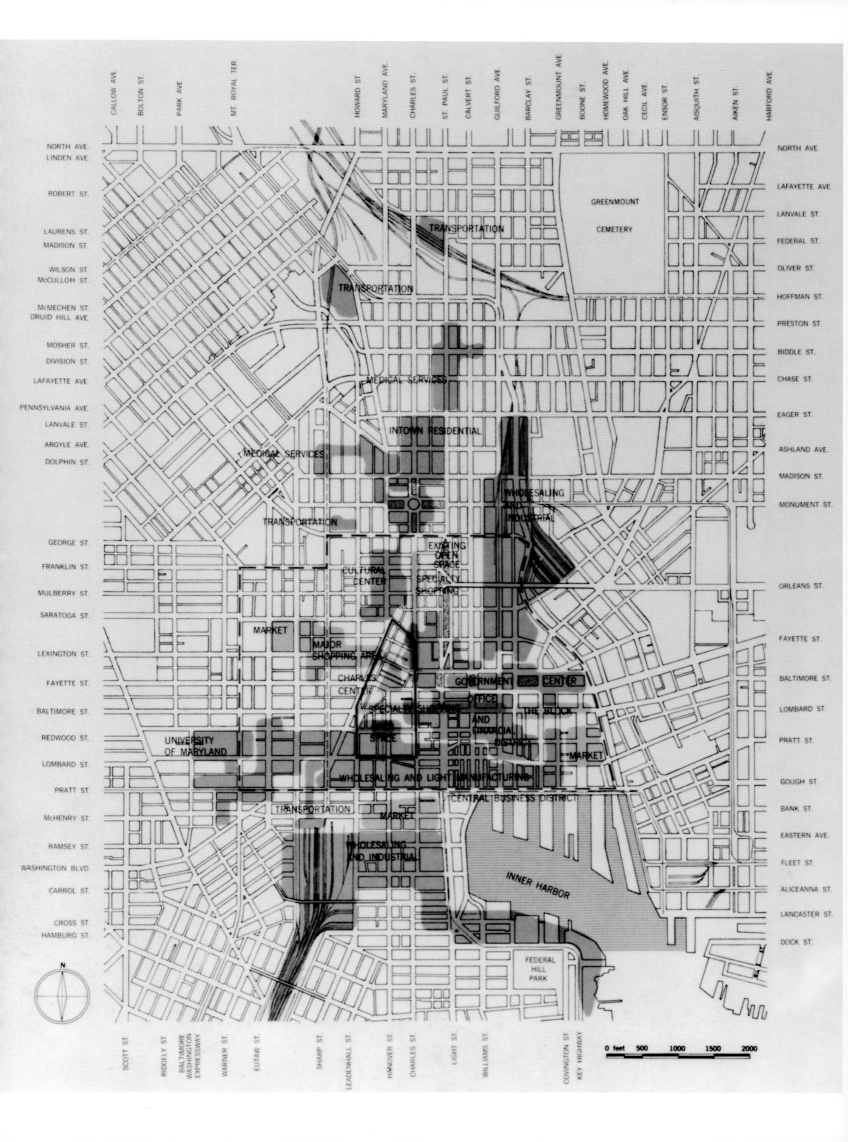

NORTH AVE.
LINDEN AVE.

ROBERT ST.

LAURENS ST.
MADISON ST.

WILSON ST.
McCULLOH ST.

McMECHEN ST.
DRUID HILL AVE.

MOSHER ST.
DIVISION ST.

LAFAYETTE AVE.

PENNSYLVANIA AVE.
LANVALE ST.
ARGYLE AVE.
DOLPHIN ST.

GEORGE ST.
FRANKLIN ST.

MULBERRY ST.
SARATOGA ST.

LEXINGTON ST.

FAYETTE ST.

BALTIMORE ST.

REDWOOD ST.

LOMBARD ST.

PRATT ST.

McHENRY ST.

RAMSEY ST.

WASHINGTON BLVD.

CARROL ST.

CROSS ST.
HAMBURG ST.

NORTH AVE.
LAFAYETTE AVE.
LANVALE ST.
FEDERAL ST.
OLIVER ST.
HOFFMAN ST.
PRESTON ST.
BIDDLE ST.
CHASE ST.
EAGER ST.
ASHLAND AVE.
MADISON ST.
MONUMENT ST.

ORLEANS ST.

FAYETTE ST.
BALTIMORE ST.
LOMBARD ST.
PRATT ST.
GOUGH ST.
BANK ST.
EASTERN AVE.
FLEET ST.
ALICEANNA ST.
LANCASTER ST.
DOCK ST.

CALLOW AVE.
BOLTON ST.
PARK AVE.
MT. ROYAL TER.
HOWARD ST.
MARYLAND AVE.
CHARLES ST.
ST. PAUL ST.
CALVERT ST.
GUILFORD AVE.
BARCLAY ST.
GREENMOUNT AVE.
BOONE ST.
HOMEWOOD AVE.
OAK HILL AVE.
CECIL AVE.
ENSOR ST.
AISQUITH ST.
AIKEN ST.
HARFORD AVE.

SCOTT ST.
RIDGELY ST.
BALTIMORE WASHINGTON EXPRESSWAY
WARNER ST.
EUTAW ST.
SHARP ST.
LEADENHALL ST.
HANOVER ST.
CHARLES ST.
LIGHT ST.
WILLIAMS ST.
COVINGTON ST.
KEY HIGHWAY

GREENMOUNT CEMETERY

TRANSPORTATION

TRANSPORTATION

MEDICAL SERVICES

INTOWN RESIDENTIAL

MEDICAL SERVICES

TRANSPORTATION

WHOLESALING AND INDUSTRIAL

EXISTING OPEN SPACE

CULTURAL CENTER

SPECIALTY SHOPPING

MARKET

MAJOR SHOPPING AREA

CHARLES CENTER

GOVERNMENT CENTER

OFFICE AND FINANCIAL DISTRICT

THE BLOCK

SPECIALTY SHOPPING

OPEN SPACE

UNIVERSITY OF MARYLAND

MARKET

WHOLESALING AND LIGHT MANUFACTURING

CENTRAL BUSINESS DISTRICT

TRANSPORTATION

MARKET

WHOLESALING AND INDUSTRIAL

INNER HARBOR

FEDERAL HILL PARK

N

0 feet   500   1000   1500   2000

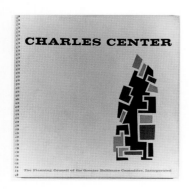

business group, the Commercial Club of
Chicago. It had hired the architect and planner Daniel Burnham to prepare a master plan
that would be offered to the city. Like the
Chicagoans, the planning council provided
factual data on why its project made sense,
and illustrations of what the new downtown
would look like. "This is Charles Center,"
the report told its readers.

> *Here, in one plan, at Downtown's Center,
> are green parks, elegant and imposing build-
> ings, convenient and adequate parking, ef-
> ficient traffic and transit, and exciting
> things to do, see, and hear. Charles Center
> is truly a contrast with the area we know
> today.[11]*

The city government was under no ob-
ligation to accept the plan, which was for-
mally presented on March 27, 1958. But the
GBC had an easy time of winning over Tho-

the watermelons that arrived each summer
to the Inner Harbor by bay boats.) In November city voters, by a wide margin, approved $25 million in bond issues to pro-
vide funds for buying properties, site clear-
ance, and any utility work (new gas, water,
electricity lines) that might be needed.

Earlier that year, as the plan was moving through all the preliminary approvals,
a delighted David Wallace remarked to a city
official on how quickly everything was hap-
pening. For most cities, delay was the norm,
he said. Getting so far in such a short time
was "just incredible."[12] In retrospect, it does
not seem so surprising. Politicians liked the
plan because this was urban renewal without much pain, there being no residential
properties within the Charles Center district.
Property owners in the urban renewal districts were assured they would get a fair price
from the city (which happened). And vot-

mas J. D'Alesandro Jr., a native of the city's
"Little Italy" and a popular and powerful
mayor. From the outset, D'Alesandro had
supported the GBC planning effort and its
attempt to emulate Pittsburgh. (He frequently
joked about how much better it would be
to have more Mellons in Baltimore than all

ers realized Baltimore had some catching up
to do. Whatever the reasons, Baltimore was
on its way.

THE CHARLES CENTER SITE

BALTIMORE REGIONS

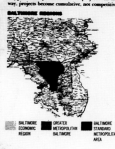

SELECTING THE SITE

Areas examined in the detailed analysis leading to the Charles Center Site.

EVERYBODY BENEFITS

ACCENTING THE POSITIVE

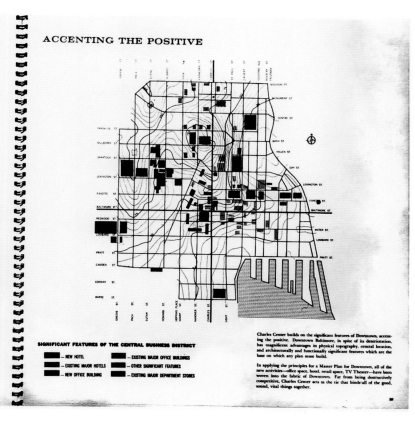

SIGNIFICANT FEATURES OF THE CENTRAL BUSINESS DISTRICT

CHARLES CENTER SITE PLAN

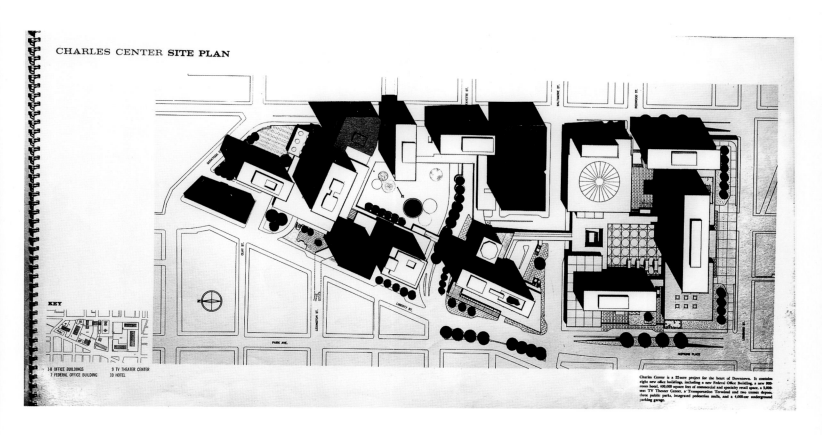

KEY

Above: The Charles Center site had a sixty-eight-foot drop from the north, at Saratoga, to the south, at Lombard Street. Topography was therefore an important element in the planning, as the map at right suggests. (Charles Center, 1958)

Below: Charles Center created space for plazas by closing off several streets, including Lexington and Redwood. (Charles Center, 1958)

*Above: The Baltimore Gas &
Electric Company Building (left),
the Lord Baltimore Hotel, and
the B&O Building (right) were
three of the five older structures
retained in the Charles Center
renewal district. (1964)*

*Left: Looking east across the site
for Charles Center. (c.1962)*

*Facing page: A building comes
down on West Baltimore Street
for the Civic Center (now the
Arena). (1960)*

Above: The Sun *Building under demolition. The B&O Building is in the background. (1964)*

Right: The south end of Charles Center. The Sun Life Insurance Company Building (right) and the George H. Fallon federal office building are underway. (1965)

II.
Charles Center

The Work Begins

Larry Smith, was a Washington real estate consultant who had done a preliminary study for the city on the feasibility of Charles Center. Smith was worried that the Baltimore Urban Renewal and Housing Agency, which was created in 1957 to coordinate urban renewal, knew more about public housing than it did about developing a new downtown commercial district. Smith urged BURHA to look for people with the necessary expertise and to create a way for them to deal directly with developers in order to cut red tape and provide confidentiality in negotiating. (All deals would be subject to final approval by the city.) The Charles Center approach became a model for many other cities. When the Inner Harbor phase began a few years later, the agency became Charles Center–Inner Harbor Management, Inc. Today the Baltimore Development Corporation serves a similar function.

From the beginning the Charles Center development office worked well, in large part because of its exceptional leadership. J. Jefferson Miller served as the first general manager. A City College and Johns Hopkins graduate who had been a naval aviator in World War I, Miller went to work at Hecht's department store in 1919 as a copywriter. He retired in 1959 as executive vice president when the May Company took over the Hecht company. Only in his early sixties and long active in the business community, Miller was persuaded to take on the Charles Center assignment. He refused to accept a

salary and signed on instead as a "dollar-a-year" man.

Dennis Durden was also an important member of the development office staff. A Georgian with a doctorate in economic geography who came on loan from Larry Smith's firm, Durden assisted Miller in getting the work underway. When Durden returned to the Smith firm in 1960, his place was taken by Martin Millspaugh, a Gilman School and Princeton graduate who was then Assistant Commissioner of the Federal Urban Renewal Administration in Washington. (During the years 1954–57 Millspaugh had covered the Charles Center story as a special writer on urban affairs for the *Baltimore Sun*).

BURHA's director was Oliver Winston, a Texan in his fifties who had worked in Washington earlier in his career and been head of Baltimore's housing agency. Richard L. Steiner, a Baltimore-raised engineer, took over in 1959. He was in charge during the implementation phase of Charles Center and served until 1968. Walter Sondheim Jr. was first chairman of BURHA. (He was succeeded by Eugene Feinblatt, an attorney who had been the author of the city's urban renewal legislation in the 1950s.) Sondheim was an executive of the Hochschild-Kohn department store and a member of a prominent merchant family in Baltimore (Isaac Hamburger was his maternal grandfather). He had already shown his ability to get Baltimoreans to pull together, as the president of the school board that implemented

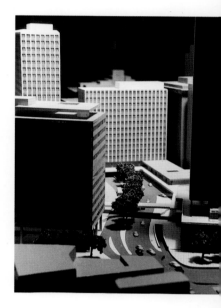

Detail of Charles Center model looking east along Fayette Street. The planned office tower over Fayette (center) was eventually replaced by the Hamburgers clothing store. It served as a link between the north and south sides of the center. (1958)

Facing page: Architects (left to right) David Scott, Al Weller, and Fred Fishback at the RTKL firm assemble the Charles Center model. (1958)

Architect David Scott and model. (1958)

Facing page: Another view of Charles Center using a photo of the model superimposed on an actual aerial photo. The final designs of most of the buildings differed from those in the model. (1958)

integration with a minimum of fuss. Sondheim was a graduate of the Park School and the class of 1929 at Haverford, the Quaker college on Philadelphia's Main Line. He had a wide range of civic contacts through his service on many boards.

In many respects, Sondheim and Miller were the linchpins in getting the project started. Sondheim knew all about government bureaucrats—he had been one himself during World War II while serving in the navy—and Miller knew all about promoting confidence in the business community. "Without Jeff, the old buildings would have come down, all right," Sondheim commented in 1964 when Charles Center was well underway. "But I don't know of any that would have gone up."[1]

In 1959 the project began in earnest when a change in federal guidelines permitted Title I dollars for downtown office projects like Charles Center. In promoting Charles Center, the city had made much of the fact that it could raise its own funds. Walter Sondheim wondered if the city wanted to continue that policy. He met with Mayor D'Alesandro, who left little doubt where he stood on the issue. "Be first in line in Washington," he told Sondheim.[2] Title I of the Housing Act and other federal programs would provide most of the public money for Charles Center and the Inner Harbor. But the costs for buying and developing sites were still the responsibility of the developer. In the case of Charles Center, the total public spending came to approximately $35 million, of which more than $20 million came from the federal government. Over $200 million in private dollars, however, eventually went into Charles Center, which was officially completed in 1986. The recycled real estate produced around $2 million a year more in taxes than the old assessments.[3]

One Charles Center

In downtown development projects, a goodly number of tenants were usually lined up in the early stages of planning, as was the case at Gateway Center in Pittsburgh. The mortgage holder (the Prudential Life Insurance Company) had a guarantee of sixty percent occupancy and twenty-year leases in its first three buildings even before ground was broken. This was the result of direct pressure from banker Richard Mellon, who told local companies that his family was not going to help Pittsburgh unless they showed their support. "It's just as simple as that," he said.[4] In Baltimore, the Charles Center Management Office had a worrisome time in the early stages because it was having little luck wooing developers, in large part because many felt Charles Center, and the first project, One Charles Center, were chancy proposals. To be sure, the office tower had a prime location on the site of O'Neill's department store, at Charles and Lexington Streets. The building was to be twenty to twenty-five stories high with between 250,000 and 275,000 square feet of office space. The building was also to include between 30,000 and 40,000 square feet of retail space and some underground parking for tenants. All of these details were in what was called the "Area 7 Prospectus" issued by the Charles Center Management Office in the name of BURHA, in November 1959. As in all the projects for Charles Center and the Inner Harbor, the city paid the cost of buying and clearing the site through bond issues and federal funds. The developer was required to purchase his site at the fair market value, in this case $800,000, and put up a building with his own or borrowed dollars.

To the relief of the Management Office, six developers showed their faith in the project by submitting formal proposals at the deadline date. One of those was Baltimorean Jacob Blaustein, the owner of Crown Central Petroleum. He wanted a new headquarters for Crown and his subsidiary companies. His architect was Marcel Breuer, a noted member of the German Bauhaus group before he emigrated to America in the 1930s. Breuer was known for his imaginative use of stone and concrete in his designs. His proposal for One Charles Center featured a precast concrete facade with recessed windows, and tree-like columns for the side facing a plaza that the planners had located next to the site. The winning developer, however, was Metropolitan Structures of Chicago, which had done many projects

around the country. It was picked in part because it had an even more prominent architect, Ludwig Mies van der Rohe, another modernist from Germany who preferred to work with metal and glass. His sleek skyscrapers epitomized the best in the International style, which was very popular at that time.

The design Mies presented for One Charles Center was a tower with a bronze-colored curtain wall, gray-tinted glass, and big plaza. If impressive, it was also something of a knock-off of his recently completed Seagram Building (1958) in New York. The Charles Center architectural review

board did not care about the similarity, given the high praise the Seagram Building received. G. Holmes Perkins, chairman of the architecture department at the University of Pennsylvania, had doubts, however, about calling One Charles Center "a major contribution to architecture," as David Wallace planned to do in a report. It was a good building, Perkins said, but there was "certainly nothing new," and he was not convinced "one more Miesian structure adds anything to architecture generally." Wallace's report read simply "a major contribution to Baltimore."[5]

Mies was, after all, Mies. As a *Sun* editorial pointed out, "His name alone guarantees for Charles Center a special national, indeed international prestige. Prestige is important to a project like Charles Center. It helps to create excitement and confidence."[6] And so it did. The Hamburgers store (1963) and Vermont Savings Bank Building (1964)—now Harbor Bank—soon followed, as did others in the 1960s, among them the Sun Life Building (1966), the Baltimore Gas and Electric addition (1966), the George H. Fallon federal office building (1967), and the Hilton (now Wyndham) Hotel (1967). The Mercantile–Safe Deposit & Trust Co. Building (1970) and Charles Center South (1975) were two major office buildings added in the next decade. By the time the project was officially completed in 1986, Charles Center had added two million square feet of office space, along with 652 apartment units, a theater, 3,000 parking spaces, and 430,000 square feet for retail.

Meeting Challenges

The first project was supposed to have been a federal office building, but the director of the General Services Administration (the agency in charge of federal properties) shared the doubts of the private developers about Charles Center. Franklin G. Floete was also unhappy about the proposed location for his building within Charles Center. It was to be tucked away on the southwest side facing what was then an industrial neighborhood. Floete preferred Charles Street, a more fashionable address and also what he considered a better real estate investment. He wanted the block between Baltimore and Lombard Streets, where the Morris A. Mechanic Theater, Sun Life Insurance, and Charles Center South now stand. Earlier in his career, Floete had been a successful businessman in everything from lumber and cattle to Ford tractors, and he still had an interest in the Floete Land and Loan Company in his hometown of Armour, South Dakota. Floete also ran the General Services Administration as though his own dollars were at stake. David Wallace, however, refused to budge. He argued that the change would wreck the plan's design and

rob it of a site that could produce tax revenues. Congressman George H. Fallon, who was a member of the House Public Works Committee, finally got Floete to agree to the Lombard Street location, no doubt part of the reason why the building bears Fallon's name.

The hotel deal also required much negotiating. Hilton was happy with Baltimore as a good place to invest since the city had only five hotels with more than two hundred beds, compared to Milwaukee's twelve or Cleveland's twenty—cities of similar size—and Baltimore had not seen a new hotel since the Lord Baltimore opened its doors in 1929. But the hotel chain was unhappy about putting up the big eight-hundred-room convention hotel that the Charles Center Management office wanted. That's too big for Baltimore, they said, pointing to the money it was losing on a new hotel of that size in Denver. A compromise allowed Hilton to put up the hotel in stages. After the first tower in 1967, another one, with 250 rooms, was finished in 1974, and a third with 221 rooms in 1981. Metropolitan Structures, which had done One Charles Center, was also the hotel's developer. It negotiated a long-term lease with an option to buy instead of having to pay immediately for the site. In addition, the city helped out with a bond issue in 1962 that permitted the hotel to borrow eighty-five percent of the cost for an underground garage. All these concessions were more or less necessary, given the uncertainty of the outcome at the time and a surrounding neighborhood that looked like London during the Blitz, with mountains of rubble everywhere as the old buildings came down.

Jacob Blaustein of Crown Central Petroleum gave the Charles Center planners a challenge of a different sort. In the fall of 1960, shortly after Metropolitan Structures had been awarded One Charles Center, Blaustein announced that he was going to go ahead with the new headquarters building that he had planned before losing the One Charles Center competition. It would be outside the Charles Center urban renewal district but just across the street from One Charles Center. For this new project, he hired Philadelphia architect Vincent F. Kling,

One Charles Center from South Charles Street. The building was designed by the prominent architect Mies van der Rohe in the sleek International style that was popular at the time. The proposal was submitted by Chicago developers who teamed with Mies. (1964)

who was skilled in designing a steel-frame building that would be required for the smaller site. At thirty stories, One North Charles was a little taller than One Charles Center but comparable in office space because its footprint was smaller. If not as dramatic as One Charles Center, it had a sleek modern design of its own.

The Charles Center Management Office was concerned about the competition for tenants since Blaustein employees were expected to fill only forty percent of the space in his new building. But Blaustein's deci-

sion was also understandable. Charles Center Management Office had put a moratorium on office buildings within the project until One Charles Center was finished, and Blaustein was unwilling to wait. To be sure, Blaustein could have leased space from Metropolitan Structures in One Charles Center, but he preferred to be an owner. During the construction period (One Charles Center and One North Charles were going up at the same time) there was much arm-twisting of potential tenants, but both buildings turned out to be successes. As for the

Charles Center master plan, an office build-ing in Development Area I was replaced with some upscale housing comparable to the Society Hill towers in Philadelphia. The housing added diversity and proved to be a hit. The first tower, with two hundred units, rented out quickly. A second with another two hundred apartments was completed in 1968.

Assessing the Plan

Architecture critic Jane Jacobs was one of the many admirers of Charles Center. She liked the project's being in the center of the city, not on the fringe; she liked the plazas; she liked the attention to the pedestrian. Jacobs had become increasingly unhappy about much of the wrecker-ball mentality of downtown urban renewal, views that would soon appear in her influential book *The Death and Life of American Cities* (1961). "Very heartfelt cheers," she told James Rouse in a letter when she was preparing an ar-ticle for *Architectural Forum*, "from someone who is so grateful to be delighted for a change, instead of depressed and disheart-ened, by a downtown project."[7]

One of the distinctive features of the Charles Center project was the decision not to raze the entire site but instead retain a few older buildings—the Lord Baltimore Hotel, a red-bricked Georgian from the 1920s, and three office buildings: the B&O Rail-road headquarters, an impressive turn-of-the-century granite monument to railroad-ing; the Fidelity and Deposit, another solid granite building that dated from the 1890s; and the Italianate Baltimore Gas and Elec-tric Company building.[8] Charles Center blended nicely into adjacent areas. The of-fice buildings were in good shape, despite their age. They would have been very ex-pensive to condemn. (At the time Charles Center was designed, it was not eligible for Title I urban renewal dollars, so everyone was also conscious of keeping down site clear-ance costs.) The office buildings also housed hundreds of office workers, and no one wanted business disrupted unnecessarily. Charles Center needed the Lord Baltimore even after a new hotel was built because Baltimore had too few rooms.

Interest in historic preservation was not a factor in the decision to save the build-ings; indeed, among architects and plan-ners in those years it was in short supply. This was the generation that had witnessed the promise of urban renewal in Europe af-ter the destruction of World War II. In their view, Downtown America was also ready for a new master plan, the streetcar city becom-

ing increasingly unable to meet the needs of the automobile age. They were not averse to saving architectural gems like the B&O building, but they were not necessarily looking for them. Whatever the motivation, saving some buildings was a plus. As Jane Jacobs remarked, Charles Center became "less of a 'project' than an integral, continuous part of downtown."[9]

Charles Center's urban renewal transformed the old midtown into three public plazas: a small one (Charles) at the north end near Saratoga Street, and two bigger ones. Center Plaza, on the north side, nearly filled an entire block. Hopkins Plaza on the south side was more intimate, with a fountain in the center. Parking garages were under the Center and Hopkins Plazas. The space

In order to provide a site big enough for the Civic Center, a superblock was created on the west side. Liberty Street, which cut through on a diagonal (in the middle of the picture), was closed off, as was Redwood Street (center). (1960)

The completed Civic Center. The serrated roof, with its pleat-like folds, gave the building a distinctive silhouette. (1962)

for the plazas was created by closing off several streets (Clay, Hopkins, Lexington, and Redwood) between Liberty and Charles. These were known as superblocks in the planning jargon of that era, the aim being to reconfigure downtown space to meet changing needs. In this instance, the idea seemed to be valid, as there were no large parks or public spaces in downtown Baltimore. The size of the Center Plaza made it appropriate for big events like the Baltimore City Fair, a popular event that drew thousands in celebration of Baltimore's neighborhoods. The first city fair was held at Center Plaza in 1970 and continued there for several years before moving to the Inner Harbor.[10] Hopkins Plaza, which was more of an amphitheater in ambiance, became a popular venue for outdoor evening concerts in the summer, a tradition that has continued over the years.

Although public in theory, the plazas tended to serve primarily the tenants of the surrounding office buildings, as William H. Potts, then the director of the GBC Planning Council, predicted in 1962. (He esti-

mated that only twenty-five percent of the plaza users would be visitors.) The plazas were not easily seen from surrounding streets, and this also kept use down. The superblocks made a dramatic change in the downtown streetscape. The Charles Center superblock eliminated a block of Lexington between Charles and Liberty that in its heyday had been a busy commercial street and a popular pedestrian route between the financial district and the department stores at Howard Street. On the west side, just outside the Charles Center urban renewal district, the Civic Center (1962) covered six acres and blocked off the south end of Liberty. This was the facility that the GBC had wanted at the Inner Harbor back in 1956 when it hired Pietro Belluschi as its consultant. (It was planned before Charles Center and funded separately.) Now everyone was willing to accept a west side location since it would help the Charles Center project. Even so, the Civic Center was still just a big box that did little for the neighborhood in terms of aesthetics.

Skywalks rimmed Charles Center and

later extended southward to the Inner Harbor. They were designed to make life easier for pedestrians by keeping them above vehicular traffic. Businesses were expected to provide services at the skywalk level to encourage their use. The Vermont Savings Bank (now Harbor Bank) had two lobbies with tellers, one on the ground level and another to serve the customers on the skywalk level. The impressive main entrance of the Morris A. Mechanic Theater was at the skywalk level, as was its lobby. Hamburgers had entrances on walkways at the front and back of the store, which was built over Fayette Street to serve as a bridge between the north and south sections of Charles Center. (Hamburger got what appeared to be a prime location, and the city got taxes on the air rights.) When the walkway was extended to the Inner Harbor, it passed through the Equitable Bank Center (1980), where Hutzler's had a small branch store adjacent to the walkway concourse.

Unfortunately, the skywalk was a design feature that did not meet with much approval, pedestrians preferring to stay at street level. With the exception of the segment through the Equitable Bank Center (now the Bank of America Center), it was outdoors and uncovered. Enclosed skywalks have been more successful in frigid climes where they offer protection for pedestrians in winter. In the 1980s, the first sections, on the north side, around the Gas and Electric Company, were dismantled. More came down in the 1990s, along with the Hamburgers store. Of the two remaining sections, one crosses Lombard Street and connects nearby hotels on the north side with Hopkins Plaza and the Mechanic Theater (which retains its skywalk lobby). The other extends from the south end of Hopkins Plaza to the Inner Harbor. It passes over the traffic on busy Pratt Street and sees a good deal of use from office workers and tourists.

With its concrete facade, jutting planes, and sharp angles, the Mechanic Theater was an impressive example of the Brutalism school of that era. It was a bit much for staid Baltimore, observed *Sun* architecture critic John Dorsey. But even if many found it ugly, Dorsey thought "most will concede that it is at least interesting looking, and a

The George H. Fallon federal office building in early stages of construction. (1965)

good deal more imaginative in design than much drab modern architecture."[11] John M. Johansen designed the theater as a sculptural piece to play off the older and more traditional styles of the Lord Baltimore Hotel and the B&O buildings across the street. The architect was hired by Morris Mechanic, a patron of Baltimore's arts and owner of Ford's, the last remaining legitimate theater downtown and badly in need of replacing. Mechanic put $4.2 million of his own money into the new theater. It opened on January 16, 1967, with a road show version of the musical *Hello Dolly*, and Betty Grable in the lead role that Carol Channing had made famous in the Broadway hit. Unfortunately Mechanic did not get to see that show; he died of a heart attack a few months before opening night.

Steelworkers atop the federal office building. The Maryland National Bank Building is in the center. The Blaustein Building is at left. (1965)

Above: Steelworkers lay the floor foundation. (1965)

Right: Looking northeast from the site of the federal office building. (1964)

Facing page: The scaffolding on the side of the federal office building contained an elevator for carrying workers and materials. (1965)

The cleared site for Charles Center created an unusual downtown perspective. The foundation of the federal office building is in the foreground. (1964)

FIRST
NATIONAL
BANK
OF
MARYLAND

NO PARKING
ANY TIME

Workers prepare for riveting . . .

. . . and pour cement. (1965)

Facing page: Workers on the side of the George H. Fallon federal office building. The view is looking east along Lombard Street. (1965)

The Plazas

At the time Charles Center was being planned, Baltimore had little in the way of parks and squares in the commercial district comparable to those in New York, Philadelphia, Washington, and many other cities. The role of the plazas of Charles Center was to address that need, and provide what William Potts, the director of the Planning Council in 1964, called a "social focus for cultural and recreational activities."

Plazas have a long and honored tradition in urban planning. They can serve as an attractive setting for civic events such as concerts or festivals, or simply as a pleasant spot to enjoy lunch with a friend. The architectural firm of Rogers, Taliaferro, Kostrisky & Lamb (RTKL) was given the assignment of designing the Charles Center plazas. It drew inspiration and ideas from many cities, both in the United States and abroad, producing such distinctive features as the Charles Center's cluster lights, which were based on a design from Venice.

The original concept called for the North Plaza (Charles) to be built around light, the Center Plaza around sculpture, and Hopkins Plaza around water. Charles still has plenty of light (an open expanse facing Charles Street) and Hopkins has its fountain. But Francesco Somaini's "Energy" sculpture, which had been donated by the Baltimore Gas & Electric Company, was later moved to a recycling facility in South Baltimore.

Each of the plazas is different in size, shape, and even elevation, as the site of Charles Center slopes sharply (sixty-eight feet) from north to south. Charles Plaza at the north is the smallest in size, but its design extends across Charles Street to include the Romanesque St. Paul's Episcopal Church, in a blend of old and new. Center Plaza is the biggest and most expansive, in the shape of an ellipse that contrasts with the angularity of the buildings surrounding it. Hopkins Plaza has proven the most popular over the years, in part because it has many places to sit and in part because of the attraction of the Jacob France fountain. But all the plazas are interesting essays in design ideas.

A woman crosses Center Plaza. The stonework is in the form of an ellipse to complement the plaza's irregular shape. (c.1970)

Facing page: The steps at Charles Plaza. (1978)

Above: Across Charles Street, St. Paul's Episcopal Church provides an attractive view and also encloses the space. (1967)

Facing page: Charles Plaza, at the corner of Saratoga and Charles Streets, presents an attractive geometric design. (1978)

Above: The cluster lights of a design found in Venice were a distinctive feature of the Charles Center plazas. (1978)

Left: Entering Charles Plaza from Charles Street. The Charles Center apartment buildings are on the left and right. (1978)

Facing page: The benches in Charles Plaza provide separate seating areas and complement the circular design of the brickwork. (1978)

Above: One Charles Center. (1961)

Left: Entrance to Center Plaza from the corner of Liberty and Lexington Streets. The view of Center Plaza opens up as one moves farther along the promenade, an approach similar to "discovering" New York's Rockefeller Plaza when entering it from Fifth Avenue. The equestrian statue represents Power. This is appropriate, given its location in front of the Gas & Electric Company building. It also brings to mind Baltimore's racing tradition at Pimlico. (c.1967)

Facing page: Construction begins on Center Plaza. (1962)

The promenade on the side of One Charles Center is a part of the skywalk plan. The new building at far right is the addition to the Baltimore Gas & Electric Company. (c.1970)

Left: A sunny afternoon at Center Plaza. A 550-car garage lies beneath the decorative stonework. (c.1970)

Facing page: Center Plaza hosts a flea market. The Hilton Hotel's first tower is in the center background. (c.1970)

Overleaf: Hopkins Plaza is an inviting public space. The main entrance to the Morris A. Mechanic Theater at the skywalk level is aligned with the Bank of America Building (right rear), and the tall columns that flank the theater entrance echo the design of that building. (1967)

57

The skywalk on the north side of Hopkins Plaza created an amphitheater ambiance for events like this concert. The view is from the George H. Fallon federal office building, which enclosed the south side of the plaza. (c.1967)

*Above: The concourse under the
skywalk at Hopkins Plaza. In
recent years parts of the
skywalk in Hopkins Plaza have
been removed. Much of this is
now open space. (c.1970)*

*Right: The pedestrians on the
right are heading for the
skywalk. (c.1970)*

The upper level of the skywalk at the Mechanic Theater. The view is to the north. The Hilton Hotel is at center left. (1967)

Above: The fountain at Hopkins Plaza. The serrated roof of the Civic Center and the Bromo Seltzer Tower provide background design elements. (1967)

Right: Enjoying a sunny day. The Mercantile–Safe Deposit & Trust Building is in the background. The cluster lights were an important design element of all the plazas. (c.1967)

Evening in Hopkins Plaza. The Sun Life Insurance Building is on the right, and the Maryland National Bank Building (now Bank of America) is in the center distance. (1967)

III.
The Inner Harbor

Adding Another Dimension

harles Center and the Inner Harbor were remarkable projects, not the least for the sheer size of their area, which recycled over 150 acres. That was more than the 140 acres destroyed in the great fire of 1904. Most of the "Burnt District," as it was officially designated, was quickly rebuilt and resumed its earlier functions. By contrast, this mid-century downtown renaissance created something quite different from what had been there before: a second new downtown area. In his inaugural address in May 1963, Mayor Theodore R. McKeldin recalled the civic response to the great fire. Once again the city was on the move, he said. Charles Center was leading the way in the private sector, but why not a new municipal center that would be "worthy of comparison with Charles Center? And why not "a new inner harbor area, where the imagination of man can take advantage of a rare gift of nature to produce an enthralling panorama of office buildings, parks, high-rise apartments, and marinas?"[1]

In effect McKeldin was re-introducing the ideas of Arthur McVoy, the planner in the 1950s whose proposal for an Inner Harbor approach had been superceded by the GBC's Charles Center plan. McKeldin had a longtime interest in city planning and in recycling the Inner Harbor in particular, having begun some of the improvements on the Light Street waterfront during his previous term as mayor in the 1940s. Most business leaders were enthusiastic, but

Jefferson Miller and Martin Millspaugh were less so because Charles Center was far from finished. McKeldin managed to win them over with the argument that there was no guarantee that a future mayor would be as supportive. David Wallace, who had returned to Philadelphia in 1961 after Charles Center was launched, came back to consult on a plan. He worked with Thomas Todd, a partner in Wallace's Philadelphia architectural firm.

The Inner Harbor plan included offices, apartments, cultural attractions, and McVoy's municipal center. Unlike the Charles Center plan, it was more a guiding vision than a blueprint. The development area was also much larger. In comparison to Charles Center's thirty-three acres, the new plan called for the development of ninety-five acres in the Inner Harbor's first phase and over a hundred later on. The time schedule was much more long-range: a twenty- to thirty-year period was expected in anticipation of projected costs and delays. But everyone was optimistic because of the potential of the Inner Harbor, which in David Wallace's apt description, "looks inward on itself, is intimate in scale, is enclosed, framed, and yet opens provocatively to the Outer Harbor and to the world."[2]

Getting Underway

The municipal center was the first project because McKeldin wanted to start there. A tree-lined plaza with courts and other

A city fair at the Inner Harbor. (c.1975)

Facing page: Along the water's edge (left to right) are Harborplace's Pratt Street Pavilion, the World Trade Center, and the National Aquarium, under construction. (c.1981)

Left: Aerial view of the lower harbor area looking southeast (1960). Right: Stevedores at work. (1956). Below: Tugs tending a freighter. (c.1970)

Aerial view of the Inner Harbor looking west. (c.1981)

Facing page: The Nippon Maru, *a Japanese training ship for naval cadets, passes a bay steamer at a Pratt Street pier. (c.1960)*

municipal buildings would run from City Hall to the Inner Harbor, in something of a grand civic promenade that would also provide a dramatic visual link between City Hall and the new waterfront. The state government in Annapolis supported the concept by agreeing to locate a new World Trade Center on the Inner Harbor at the south end of the proposed plaza. The Inner Harbor–Municipal Center plan, as it was called, was officially released by McKeldin in September of 1964, with much of the same hoopla when the Charles Center was announced in 1958. As was the case with Charles Center, voters had to approve some bond issues to get the work underway. It was decided to move quickly and put the Municipal Center proposals on the November ballot. This proved to be a mistake as voters rejected all the bonds. The *Evening Sun* found it "puzzling and disturbing" because it felt the city badly needed a new municipal center.[3]

The defeat was not that surprising, given the widespread criticism about the lack of detailed information on the proposals, which included a new headquarters for school administrators, a new municipal court and new police station. The business community had also not been as prepared

for selling the voters as it had been with Charles Center. In the summer of 1964 when the plan was being completed, David Barton, the advertising executive who had supervised the 1958 publicity booklet, had suggested a similar campaign for the Inner Harbor bonds. Boucher, the GBC's executive director, agreed it was a good idea, but delays at the GBC kept the finished report from being ready until after the bond vote. In some respects, this reflected overconfidence at the outcome. It would also be fair to say that the business community was lukewarm at best about the Municipal Center aspects of the Inner Harbor plan, given its own focus on renewing the business district.

Shortly after the vote in 1964, McKeldin announced that the emphasis would indeed now be on commercial aspects of the Inner Harbor, in the vicinity of Pratt and Light Streets, where developers had shown an interest. Boucher later said that the defeat of the municipal center loans might have been "a good thing." If planning had started with the public buildings there, "We would have been a long time getting to Pratt and Light, and this is really the heart of the project."[4]

The next chance to put the Inner Harbor plan before the voters was in November of 1966. A Citizens Committee for the Inner Harbor Loan was created, with Walter Sondheim Jr. as chairman. This time, the GBC relied on flyers, to some 200,000 registered voters (or approximately half of city voters) in precincts where the vote on bond issues was usually heavy. Another 100,000 pieces of literature were given to organizations that ranged from the League of Women Voters to the Baltimore Council of the AFL-CIO. Endorsements were secured from all the major civic and professional associations as well as a host of politicians. Ads supporting the Inner Harbor appeared in the city's major papers as well as the *Afro-American* and the *Catholic Review*. Boucher appeared with the mayor on a special fifteen-minute presentation on the plan aired by WJZ-TV on the night before the vote. The bond issue passed by a two-to-one majority.

The Charles Center–Inner Harbor Management, Inc., a nonprofit corporation that had been created in 1965, was in charge of the planning. As the name suggests, it was

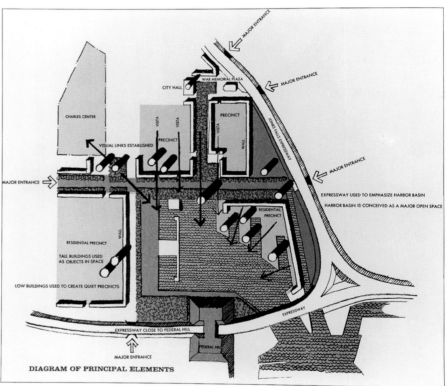

DIAGRAM OF PRINCIPAL ELEMENTS

Left: A model of how the Inner Harbor might look after redevelopment. The cross-harbor expressway (I-95) and the extension of the Jones Falls Expressway (I-83) into Fells Point were separate federal projects. Both were later rejected by the city. From Inner Harbor Report, published by the Greater Baltimore Committee and the Committee for Downtown. (1965) Top: A view of the model from the east. The tall buildings on the city piers on Pratt Street (center) are apartments that planners hoped developers would build. Some later went up at other locations around the Inner Harbor. (Inner Harbor Report, 1965) Below: Diagram showing visual linkages between midtown and the Inner Harbor. A mall between City Hall and the Inner Harbor (upper center) was dropped after voters rejected bond issues.

Right: The old Otterbein Methodist Church. Built in 1785, it is the second oldest church in Baltimore. It is now nearly surrounded by the recent addition to the Convention Center. (1966)

Below: İndustrial neighborhoods of South Baltimore. Most of the warehouses and other properties on the far left were cleared for an expressway link to downtown and a site for a new Federal Reserve building. (c.1971)

Top row: Camden Station (left) before it was restored to its original design. The station now has towers at either end and on the main building (left center). (1970) The Roosevelt Hotel, right (the Joyce for most of its years), was located across the street from Camden Station. (1970)

(Middle row): Fava Fruit warehouse (left) on South Charles has an impressive cast-iron facade (1969). Nearby Light Street (right) also had many warehouses (1969).

(Left): A can factory and warehouse at Charles and Barre Streets (1969). Harbor Court hotel and apartments are now on the site.

The Church of the Lord Jesus Christ of Apostolic Faith on South Sharp Street. It survived all the urban renewal changes. (1970)

an expansion of the Charles Center management operation. Miller and Millspaugh now oversaw both projects. Miller, still the "dollar-a-year" man, agreed to complete Charles Center as general manager. Millspaugh became the salaried president and general manager of the Inner Harbor projects and the person primarily responsible for that operation.[5]

A lot of offices were built in the early years because of the strong interest among developers and potential tenants. United States Fidelity & Guaranty Company, a big insurer, moved from Calvert Street to a new headquarters tower (1973) at Light and Pratt Streets. The thirty-six-story building (now the Legg Mason Tower) was the first office building for the Inner Harbor. The USF&G building was an important design link between Charles Center and the Inner Harbor. Its spacious plaza served as a transition space between the two projects. The tall glass walls on the ground floor also provided sightlines through the lobby toward the Inner Harbor. Other offices included the IBM building (1975) and the Chesapeake and Potomac Telephone Company headquarters in the Constellation Place project (1977) on the southwest corner of Light and Pratt Streets. Like Charles Center, the Inner

Harbor also got a big federal building, the Edward A. Garmatz (1976) courthouse, which filled a block between Lombard and Pratt Streets directly south of Charles Center. And even though the city failed to build the municipal plaza, the state went ahead with the World Trade Center (1977). The impressive twenty-eight-story building has an observation deck at the twenty-seventh floor and a pentagonal shape that suggests the prow of a ship on the harbor side.

Housing

Most of the housing in the Inner Harbor plan had been envisioned as upscale units in soaring towers along waterfront piers. This made sense because the Inner Harbor seemed like a natural site for attracting the affluent who would boost the tax base and spend money downtown. Developers, however, were hesitant to test that market until restaurants, marinas, and other amenities were part of the Inner Harbor atmosphere. As a result, the first Inner Harbor housing came in 1974 at the low end, with a nine-story, 291-unit apartment building for the elderly on South Light Street in what was then a racially mixed, working-class neighborhood. It was built by the Christ Lutheran Church, with the help of federal funds. The apartment building was part of a larger complex that included a 220-bed medical center and nursing home. Upscale housing came later when the Inner Harbor had more attractions. The later luxury high-rises included the Towers at Harbor Court (1986) on Light Street and Lee, Scarlett Place (1987) on East Pratt, and Harborview (1993) on Key Highway. Rentals and sales were a challenge at the outset, in part because Baltimore had never been much of an apartment city. Attractive suburban neighborhoods were close and an easy drive from downtown. An executive with Scarlett Place's development company felt confident that they would have made a fortune if Scarlett Place had been built on the Potomac River in Washington, D.C. "It's just Baltimore," he said.[6]

Row houses and townhouses had better luck. In the Otterbein neighborhood, a few blocks west of the Inner Harbor, the city had one hundred or so condemned row houses on its hands as the result of a change in plans in routing an interstate through Baltimore. In 1975 it put the houses up for sale at a dollar apiece. Participants had to pay for all the necessary repairs (which averaged around $36,000), but they were eligible for low-interest city loans. The only other major provision was that they had to live on the property for at least three years. The success of the project caught the attention of developers, who added new townhouses. And so Otterbein got a new lease on life.

The same was true for the row house communities of Federal Hill and Fells Point. They also had been in the path of the interstate project. In 1967 residents organized a preservation society to save the communities. As part of its publicity campaign, the society hosted its first Fells Point festival in October of that year. "The colorful and historic Fells Point–South Broadway area of Baltimore was rediscovered yesterday, and perhaps in time to save it from being wiped out by the East-West Expressway," WJZ-TV commented in an editorial that proved to be prophetic.[7] In December 1968, Mayor Thomas D'Alesandro III, the son of the former mayor, told highway officials (opponents called them the "Road Gang") to find a route that would leave the Inner Harbor alone.

Tourism

Like other cities in the so-called "rust belt" of the Northeast and Midwest, Baltimore was battered in the 1970s by competition from foreign countries, the Sun Belt, and even its own suburbs. Mayor William Donald Schaefer recognized the potential of tourism and the convention business as new sources of revenue. He pushed hard for those programs in his many years as mayor (1971–86). An important addition was a new Convention Center (1979) on West Pratt Street, built with the help of a $35 million state bond issue that voters had approved in 1975. It was sorely needed, the Arena being poorly designed to handle this assignment.

The Maryland Science Center (1976) was the first of the tourist attractions. It suc-

ceeded in making science more accessible through such innovations as interactive exhibits. The building was designed by Edward Durel Stone. Some observers criticized the windowless exterior and hint of turrets and towers, saying they reflected a patrician fear of a surrounding neighborhood that had not yet been completely gentrified. A kinder assessment would be that the Science Center had kinship with the Smithsonian Institution's gothic "castle" on the Mall in Washington. In any event, later modifications of the exterior included an inviting entrance facing the Inner Harbor. The Science Center is owned by the Maryland Academy of Sciences, a scholarly group that was founded in 1797. For years it had been making do with space on the third floor of the main branch of the Enoch Pratt Free Library. Members longed for an impressive new home, like the one Philadelphia had built for the Franklin Institute in the 1930s. When the academy started its campaign in the 1960s, it emphasized the educational benefits for the community, but the GBC's Planning Council also saw the project's tourist potential. The city donated the land, and the

Baltimore "arabbers" sold produce from horse-drawn carts. This is an arabber's stable on South Hanover Street. (1970)

Above: A storefront church on Sharp Street. (1969)

Left: The alley behind the arabber's stable, on South Hanover Street. (1970)

A parking lot at the corner of Pratt and Charles Streets; one of the many sites awaiting the redevelopment of the Inner Harbor. (c.1970)

Right: The McCormick Building on Light Street. The spice company occupied this location for more than sixty years. (c.1970)

St. Joseph Catholic Church on Lee Street, between Hanover and Sharp Streets in the Otterbein neighborhood. This block was spared when the Inner Harbor expressway plans changed. Not so the church, which had once been the Lee Street Baptist Church. It was replaced by housing during redevelopment. (1970)

The floors go up on the USF&G Building. In the center a new headquarters for First National Bank of Maryland is also under construction. (c.1973)

Top: One of Fava Fruit Company's warehouses was near the Pratt Street piers and the city's produce market. (1962)

Middle: A block on Pratt Street awaits demolition. (1962)

Left: Store reflecting the maritime focus of Pratt Street in an earlier era. (1962)

85

The elevator core of the USF&G Building. This was constructed first and the office space added around it. (1971)

state provided a $2 million grant. Another $2 million was raised by the academy.

The National Aquarium at Baltimore (1981) was also designed with tourists in mind. City officials had been intrigued by the success of Boston's New England Aquarium, which had been a part of that city's waterfront renewal. They hired the Cambridge Seven, the architectural firm that designed the New England Aquarium. Peter Chermayeff gave Baltimore a wrap-around tank that permitted visitors to see from the inside rather than from the outside, as in the Boston aquarium. He also added a rain-forest exhibit at the top of the building. The exterior of the National Aquarium was dramatically different from the Boston aquarium. It looked like outdoor sculpture, with brightly colored panels in an abstract design and a modernist triangular shape, and became as much a hit as the exhibits inside.

The "National" in the aquarium's name reflected a marketing coup for the city's tourism office. The title "National Aquarium" belonged officially to a small collection of fish tanks in the basement of the Department of Commerce building in Washington. Marylanders lobbied to get Congress to approve the name "National Aquarium in Baltimore" in November 1979. When questioned about the legislation shortly before the Senate approved it, U.S. Senator Charles Mathias said, "The designation as a national aquarium need not be exclusively reserved to the Baltimore aquarium, but could also be granted to other institutions of similar stature and function upon nomination and consideration by Congress."[8] The bill caused a mild stir at the time, but James S. Kepley, the director of the aquarium, asserted that the up-to-date facilities justified the "national" title. The aquarium has tried to keep up-to-date. A Marine Mammal Pavilion was added in 1990. It featured a million-gallon tank and a 1,300-seat amphitheater providing live shows similar to those at San Diego's Sea World.

The Hyatt Regency (1981) was the first of the Inner Harbor hotels. Its story was similar to the Hilton's in Charles Center in that dollars were necessary to coax reluctant developers who were concerned that few

The USF&G Building goes up as a neighbor comes down. (c.1972)

tourist attractions had yet been built. In 1978 the city lent $10 million from a federal Urban Development Action Grant to Hyatt, along with $2 million from other sources. With that financing in place, Hyatt was able to secure a $20 million loan from Equitable Life Insurance Company. By the end of the negotiations, the owners of the Hyatt chain had to put up only $4 million of corporate money for the $37.5 million project. The city's help caused a stir at the time, but there was little likelihood that the hotel would have gone ahead without it, and the deal negotiated by Millspaugh and BURHA's Feinblatt required that the Hyatt repay the city loan with interest before any profits could be distributed to the private owners.

Harborplace

By the late 1970s, Martin Millspaugh felt that the Inner Harbor needed what he called "the missing ingredient"—a place that served food and drink and would be interesting enough to keep people coming all year round.[9] To be sure, the Maryland Science Center was a year-round attraction at that time, but it provided little food service. The only tourist spot near the Inner Harbor fitting Millspaugh's description was the McCormick spice factory on Light Street, which featured a tea room. The company had remained as one of the last Inner Harbor sites awaiting recycling, although it was then in the midst of transferring operations to suburban Hunt Valley. (The Light Street building was demolished in the late 1980s.) McCormick offered refreshments at its teahouse, which was part of a mock Elizabethan village called "Friendship Court" on the seventh floor of the factory. Company president C. P. McCormick had installed it in the 1930s to provide a welcoming atmosphere for business visitors. Around 1950 the company included the "Friendship Court" in its factory tours. By the late 1970s some 30,000 visitors a year were sipping tea and munching cookies in Ye Olde McCormick Tea House. The tour in fact became so popular that the company stopped publicizing it because it could not handle all the group requests.

Millspaugh wanted something that would be as popular. He turned to James Rouse, who had been involved in an urban renewal project in Boston with architect Benjamin Thompson. They had taken the three imposing buildings of the historic Quincy Market, itself once a part of a neighborhood revitalization plan back in the 1820s, and turned them into a new kind of mall. The market did not include any department stores but rather a mix of upscale shops and restaurants that would appeal to tourists and suburban visitors as well as downtown office workers. They added free outdoor entertainment and cart vendors selling crafts in an informal and appealing

Facing page: The completed USF&G Building. At left is Allfirst Bank. The two buildings awaiting demolition are on Hanover Street. The view is to the east. (c.1975)

Below: Picture-taking at the newly restored U.S.S. Constellation. The sloop-of-war was returned to its berth in 1999 after extensive restoration work at a dry dock at nearby Locust Point. (1999)

The Inner Harbor before Harborplace serving as the site of an Italian festival, one of many ethnic festivals held there. The USF&G Building is at the upper left center. The McCormick spice factory is still present, opposite the boats at left. (1977)

91

mix that worked well in the old granite buildings. Taking its name from another historic structure nearby, the Faneuil Hall Marketplace was an instant hit when it opened in August 1976. It became in effect the first of a new breed that would be called the "downtown festival mall." Located between the new Government Center and the New England Aquarium, it also fulfilled its role in the overall urban renewal scheme by pulling big crowds from both directions.

Rouse was skeptical about a festival mall in Baltimore because of the two sites that Millspaugh had in mind: the turn-of-the-century Power Plant on Pratt Street, and the Camden railroad station, near the B&O Warehouse on the west side. Rouse felt both were too far from the center of downtown activity. In his view, the only location that would work was the busy corner of Light and Pratt Streets. His choice proved controversial because part of the site was a small patch of greenery with the statue of a hero of the War of 1812 in the middle. General Sam Smith Park had been there since 1950, as the result of clearing old wharves and warehouses from the Light Street waterfront. Despite early assumptions that the space would yield to more permanent plans when the recycling of the Inner Harbor got underway, the little park had taken on a permanence of its own.

Walter Sondheim Jr. recalled that the Charles Center–Inner Harbor management office unwittingly abetted the idea by sprucing up the park a bit at the time Rouse was considering the site. It had done so at the request of Mayor Schaefer, who had complained that it was becoming an eyesore. "I didn't say make it beautiful," the mayor fumed, a bit of hyperbole regarding the park's appearance but a remark that suggested how sensitive the issue had become.[10] It took a referendum to get the project moving.

Rouse and Thompson included much of the same mix of shops and restaurants they had in Boston. In Baltimore, however, they had no historic structures to provide instant atmosphere, but their airy pavilions suggested the old steamboat terminals that had once lined the Inner Harbor. Metal stairways, inside and out, enhanced the nautical theme. Harborplace was a big hit from

the day it opened in 1980, and Rouse found himself on the cover of *Time* magazine the following year.

To be sure, Harborplace had its critics. They said the festival hall concept was bogus urbanism compared to places like the Lexington and Cross Street Markets, which had been on the west and south sides of downtown respectively since the city's early years. Despite their location, they had the ambiance of a farmers' market, with lots of stalls, colorful vendors, and a diverse clientele, many of whom were inner-city minorities. By contrast, said the critics, Harborplace was just another mall for tourists and suburbanites. To some extent, this was true. But Rouse's charge was to bring new vitality to downtown by attracting more visitors who would create more jobs and revenue for the city. Viewed from this perspective, Harborplace succeeded admirably.

Above: The IBM Building's twenty-eight-story addition, with its nautical rigging at the top, rises above Harborplace's Pratt Street Pavilion. The bow of the Constellation *is at left. (1999)*

Facing page: Visitors enjoying the view from the Harborplace Pavilion on Light Street. The Pratt Street Pavilion is across the plaza. (c.1980)

IV.
Epilogue
Meeting New Challenges

The center of the new downtown today is in the vicinity of Light and Pratt Streets. Harborplace put the location on the map in 1980, but the building that did the most to firmly anchor it there was the nearby Gallery at Harborplace (1988). The Rouse Company project combined a small upscale mall (136,000 feet) with an office tower and hotel. It is located across the street from the Pratt Street Pavilion of Harborplace and is connected by an overhead walkway. The site had been originally reserved for a new building for the Federal Reserve, but the banking agency later chose a larger one on Conway and Sharp Streets near Camden Yards. The change was fortuitous because the Rouse project made better use of the block in terms of enhancing the Inner Harbor's attractions.

Like the Harborplace pavilions, the Gallery has a festival mall. There are no department stores but an abundance of shops and boutiques as well as a food hall on an upper level overlooking the Inner Harbor. The Toronto architectural firm of Zeidler Roberts designed the building. They resisted a "big box" approach and gave each of its components a distinctive exterior design. The mall, at the corner of Calvert and Pratt Streets, has an angular glass facade at its main entrance, suggesting the prow of a ship. In many respects, the Gallery complex is a composite of the design elements of the Inner Harbor: office space for businessfolk, hotel space for tourists, and restaurants and retail shopping that provide an attraction for both, as well as for suburbanites in town for the day.

In recent years that synergy has been spreading to the south side of the Inner Harbor, to Federal Hill and Locust Point, where industrial sites are being recycled. A luxury hotel has been proposed for a waterfront location near Federal Hill park. Nearby the American Visionary Museum (1995) promotes what could be called contemporary folk art. Farther down Key Highway, the Baltimore Museum of Industry has undergone an expansion. The city would like to see more tourists head in this direction. To encourage them, a shoreline promenade has been built, with private and public funds, around the Inner Harbor to the Federal Hill attractions and the Baltimore Museum of Industry. At the west end of Pratt Street, the B&O Museum is promoting its impressive collection of train equipment at its historic Mount Clare repair yards. Oriole Park at Camden Yards (1993) incorporates an eight-story, three-hundred-yard-long warehouse that had been part of the B&O freight yards. The Baltimore Ravens football stadium (1998) is much larger and modern in design, but it manages to complement Oriole Park by also using brick in its design.

The Pratt Street Corridor

Overall, more growth has taken place on East Pratt, in no small part due to John Paterakis, the owner of H&S Bakery. Paterakis became a developer after making a fortune

Facing page: The new office corridor along Pratt Street. The view is east from near Howard Street. The five-story cast-iron façade at left is one of the few that has been saved in downtown. It is now part of the modern Marsh & McLennan Building (1990) that stands behind it. (1996)

by turning a small family business into a giant operation that supplies bread to supermarkets and 2.4 billion hamburger buns a year to McDonald's restaurants on the East Coast and elsewhere. Paterakis is recycling an area of over twenty acres, which is nearly the size of Charles Center. It is located south of Little Italy, or midway between the Inner Harbor and Fells Point. He began development in 1996 with the Sylvan Learning Center, a six-story building on the waterfront, and an adjoining eleven-story apartment building, the Promenade at Inner Harbor East.

The most recent project in Inner Harbor East is a thirty-one-story Marriott hotel. This was much criticized for various reasons, from being too tall for the neighborhood to being in the wrong part of downtown. The latter issue proved to be very controversial. As it had done with earlier hotel developers, the city provided Paterakis with public subsidies through grants and tax relief. Many felt a hotel closer to the Convention Center on the west side would have been a better choice. It was not altogether clear, however, that the right developer at the right location would materialize, and Mayor Kurt L. Schmoke (1987–99) stood behind Paterakis. In any event, even the naysayers admit that the new Marriott provides a dramatic addition to downtown.

David Cordish's development company has been luring tourists to the east side with a mixed-use complex in the Power Plant that had been saved in the 1960s. This was one of the sites that Rouse had rejected in his search for a site for Harborplace, in part

Above: The Gallery complex (1988) includes a hotel, mall, and office tower. The view is to the west along Pratt Street. (1996)

Facing page: The Gallery complex under construction (c.1987).

The Hyatt was the first hotel in the Inner Harbor. It is directly across from the Light Street Pavilion of Harborplace. (1996)

because of the problems of creating a festival hall in the power plant's cavernous spaces. An amusement park company tried and failed, leaving it unused since 1987. Cordish found tenants that could put the big interior to good use, like ESPN Zone (a sports bar and restaurant), Barnes & Noble, and the Hard Rock Café. Port Discovery (1998), a children's museum, is another recent addition that is bringing the younger set to this part of Pratt Street. Designed by a Disney company, it features interactive exhibits. Like the Maryland Science Center and the National Aquarium, the museum is run by a nonprofit organization.

Farther east, and just beyond the central business district, is Fells Point. It has

become a major destination point for suburbanites as well as tourists, in part for its numerous pubs, restaurants and funky shops, but also because of its charm as an old seaport. Fells Point was designated an historic district in the 1960s, thanks to opponents of the interstate expressway. Saving Fells Point proved to be a plus for Baltimore as tourism became more important. In recent years, development has moved beyond Fells Point to Canton, an old industrial district on the waterfront. With the east-west tourist corridor over a mile in length, Mayor Schmoke proposed a monorail system in 1998 that would provide service from Camden Yards through the upper Inner Harbor to Fells Point and Canton.

The idea faces a doubtful future, given the high costs, but it suggests how much and how far the downtown renaissance has spread.

The Challenge of Midtown

What about midtown Baltimore? In recent years only eight percent of the capital investment in downtown has gone there, so it has clearly lagged behind the Inner Harbor (and the University of Maryland complex on the West Side) in terms of economic development. Office occupancy has become a game of one-way musical chairs. Some firms have moved from the old financial district to Charles Center and then to the Inner Harbor, others directly from the financial district to the Inner Harbor. This has left midtown without tenants, and they have been difficult to find. In 1997 Laurie Schwartz, the president of the Downtown Partnership business group, called it a problem of the "two downtowns." "Pratt Street may have the high buildings and the high occupancy," she said. Midtown's high vacancies, however, were "casting a shadow on downtown's future."[1]

Midtown's tourist attractions, however, are still going strong. In recent years, the Mechanic Theater has enjoyed a successful partnership with a New York company, Jujamcyn Theaters and Productions, which owns five New York theaters and manages five others across the country. Jujamcyn was interested in the Mechanic because of its reputation as one of the country's most popular theaters for touring companies. For years Hope Quackenbush (booking shows) and Sandy Hillman (publicity) played leadership roles after the city took over the theater in 1976 and created the Baltimore Center for the Performing Arts as a city-subsidized agency.

To be sure, the Mechanic Theater has presented some challenges, like the lack of backstage space and a rotating stage. In the planning phase, the Charles Center architectural review board noted these deficiencies but felt changes were unnecessary at the time. And Morris Mechanic, who funded the project and hoped to see it a profitable business investment, was understandably concerned about rising costs. In the mid-1970s the city spent $500,000 on improving acoustics and doubling the size of the orchestra pit. But the theater's relatively small size makes it hard to book big Broadway shows that have elaborate sets and high fixed costs. Even so, the theater continues to find a loyal audience.

Midtown also has the Walters Art Museum, the Peabody Conservatory, the Maryland Historical Society, the Washington Monument, and an array of shops and restaurants in the historic Mount Vernon district. A bit farther north are Center Stage, the Meyerhoff Symphony Hall, and the Lyric Opera House. The Walters draws the largest numbers, particularly during major exhibitions; 113,000 visitors came to see a Monet show, for example, during a two-month period in 1997. The total attendance that year was around 300,000, also an impressive figure, but less so compared to the number of visitors to the Inner Harbor. The Maryland Science Center had over 500,000 visitors in 1997, and the National Aquarium had 1.6 million.

The disparity in numbers between midtown and the Inner Harbor is due in part to a widespread assumption among visitors that all Baltimore's tourist attractions are at the Inner Harbor. The phalanx of office towers along Pratt Street has something to do with this. To be sure, the IBM building and others have their visual appeal, but they also suggest that the new downtown is the only downtown. One block to the north, Lombard Street reinforces this impression. With its barren streetscape (mostly parking garages for the Pratt Street office buildings, hotels, restaurants and stores) Lombard has the look of a boundary or "edge," as Kevin Lynch uses the term in his classic study *The Image of the City* (1960). The heavy traffic on Pratt and Lombard Streets is another deterrent for pedestrians who might want to venture up to midtown. Each street has five lanes in the vicinity of Harborplace, and crossing them can be a daunting experience.[2]

In the early 1960s, in the era of federal funding for interstate highways, the city had a chance to solve the problem by building an elevated cross-town expressway along the Inner Harbor near Pratt Street. It would

The Harborview apartment complex near Federal Hill. (1993)

have kept through traffic off the local streets and helped to make downtown more accessible to suburbanites and tourists, much like the expressway that passes above the Circular Quay in Sydney. But the Planning Commission's idea proved controversial, and soon all proposals were killed. A tunnel under Pratt Street is a possibility but only in theory, given the discouraging example of Boston, which built an overhead expressway in the 1960s and is now replacing it with an underground one. The Kennedy magic secured billions in federal dollars for the project, but even that has not been enough, leaving the city and state to cope with the massive overruns.

In any event, Pratt Street is a problem, and particularly so for midtown retailers, who could use more foot traffic from the Inner Harbor. Sales have suffered from suburban competition. Indeed Howard Street, once the city's main shopping venue, has lost all its department stores. Hamburgers was the only large store willing to take a gamble on the future of retailing in midtown when it signed up for Charles Center. Its decision was based more on Isaac Hamburger's commitment to seeing the project succeed than any hard marketing data. The store remained in business until 1992. Most other clothing retailers in the Charles Center area had gone years before.

Restaurants have not fared much better. Miller Brothers moved into the Hilton when the hotel was built on its former location. The restaurant survived until the early 1980s, but the old ambiance was not there, nor ultimately were the customers. Some fast-food shops were added to Charles Plaza at the upper end of Charles Center in 1985, but they face an uncertain future.

If "location, location, location" is indeed fundamental to real estate, that may explain why New York's Rockefeller Center has been such a success since it was created in the 1930s. It chose a spot between swank Fifth Avenue and Broadway's theater district, both of which helped it to draw visitors. In its design, Charles Center had a comparable mix of office buildings, restaurants, retail, and entertainment—and a similar goal of being a lively new center for downtown—but it did not get much help from the surrounding neighborhoods. The GBC's planning council might have been better off in heeding Arthur McVoy's advice to head directly for the Inner Harbor and leave midtown alone. Old neighborhoods near downtown have become a popular spot for tourists and office workers alike in Seattle and other cities that still have them. If midtown had been spruced up as McVoy suggested, with pedestrian malls and other amenities, instead of much of it being knocked down, it might well have become Baltimore's version of Old Town—full of quaint shops, cafes, and historic architecture that would have nicely complemented the glitz of the Inner Harbor.

Recent Renewal

But all is not gloom and doom in midtown—far from it. In recent years, Charles Center has acquired a new lease on life, in no small part due to the leadership of Peter Angelos, the Baltimore attorney who made a fortune in asbestos litigation. Angelos bought and renovated One Charles Center and is using it as a headquarters for his law firm. Across the street, on the site of Hamburgers, the Johns Hopkins University has built a new continuing education center. A few blocks south on Charles Street, the Hansa Haus, erected in 1912 as an office building for a German steamship company, has been restored by Allfirst Bank, which is using it for brokerage offices. The bank's main office building is a block south on Charles Street.

Over on Light Street between Baltimore and Redwood, a block that has not seen building activity in decades, a new hotel is underway where the Southern Hotel once stood. The old financial district is also attracting new interest for its architectural gems. At the corner of Baltimore and Calvert Streets the venerable Alex. Brown building, which dates from 1904 and survived the Great Fire that year, has been lovingly restored by the Chevy Chase Bank. The bank opened a branch there after the brokerage firm moved its headquarters to a nearby office tower. In Mount Vernon, the Maryland Historical Society is expanding its gallery space, as has the Walters Art Gallery, which recently completed a major renovation. And to help visitors to see these and other attractions in midtown, the Downtown Partnership has plans for a tourist bus up Charles Street which will connect Mount Vernon with the Inner Harbor.

As Baltimore enters the new century, it is stunning how much downtown has changed since the 1950s. To be sure, some cherished landmarks disappeared, like the imposing *Sun* building on Charles Street with its impressive colonnades, or the graceful rotunda of Metropolitan Savings Bank up the street at Saratoga, or the tobacco warehouses near the Inner Harbor. The narrow block of Lexington between Liberty and Charles, filled with shops in its heyday, was a lively bit of streetscape that was lost, as well as most of Baltimore's cast-iron heritage. But it also must be remembered that Baltimore faced the crisis of a changing economy. Urban renewal was part of the response that inevitably changed the look of downtown, just as the Industrial Revolution in the nineteenth century changed the landscape of the early Baltimore we see in Strickland's engraving. In return, Baltimore got some lovely new buildings, some lively new districts, and a new appreciation for the natural beauty of the Inner Harbor. Always a livable city, Baltimore lives on.

The new Inner Harbor from Federal Hill. The memorial at left commemorates General George Armistead, who defended Baltimore in the War of 1812. (1996)

References

Chapter One

[1] Fells Point is not in the Strickland picture, so we do not have a full view of Baltimore as a port at that time. Founded a few years earlier than Baltimore, and a bit farther down the bay, it handled bigger ships because of its deeper water. It became a part of Baltimore in 1797.

[2] Planning Council of the Greater Baltimore Committee. Draft of retail trade report (1958), series 6, box 2, Greater Baltimore Committee Collection, Special Collections, Langsdale Library, University of Baltimore (hereinafter cited as GBC Collection).

[3] As part of his on-going interest in the housing problem, Rouse created the Enterprise Foundation in the 1980s. It is involved in rehabbing old homes and building new ones in inner-city neighborhoods. Rouse died in 1995.

[4] GBC, *Annual Report* (1955), series 1, box 1, GBC Collection.

[5] Excerpts of Kiwanis Club speech in letter to James A. Linen [publisher of *Time* magazine], August 18, 1955, series 3, GBC Collection.

[6] *Baltimore Sun,* July 16, 1956.

[7] Planning Council, "Report and Recommendation on the Civic Center to the Greater Baltimore Committee," [February 1957], series 6, box 24, GBC Collection.

[8] Planning Council, "Staff Meeting—Discussion of Progressive Planning," September 5, 1957, series 7, box 14, GBC Collection.

[9] Wallace, "The Planning Process," in Martin Millspaugh, ed., *Baltimore's Charles Center: A Case Study in Downtown Renewal* (Washington, D.C.: Urban Land Institute, 1964), 16.

[10] Planning Council *Minutes* (March 6, 1958), series 14, GBC Collection.

[11] *Charles Center* (Baltimore: The Greater Baltimore Committee, 1958), 1.

[12] Wallace to Oliver Winston, June 24, 1958, series 6, box 11, GBC Collection.

Chapter Two

[1] *Baltimore Sun*, October 18, 1964.

[2] Author interview with Walter Sondheim, February 14, 1994.

[3] In some instances the city allowed developers to lease the land. It also would not sell any land that had once been a public park, as was the case later on in the Inner Harbor.

[4] Michael P. Weber, *Don't Call Me Boss: David Lawrence, Pittsburgh's Renaissance Mayor* (Pittsburgh: University of Pittsburgh Press, 1988), 162.

[5] Letter from Perkins to Wallace (April 18, 1960) and report are in series 6, box 20, GBC Collection.

[6] *Baltimore Sun*, May 6, 1960.

[7] "A New Heart for Baltimore," *Architectural Forum* (June 1958): 88–92; Jacobs to Rouse, March 31, 1958, series 6, box 17, GBC Collection.

[8] The Charles Center planners also saved a fifth structure, albeit reluctantly. This was the Rennert garage, which had recently gone up on the site of the old Rennert Hotel at the corner of Liberty and Saratoga Streets. It provided some parking for Charles Center, but it was not an architectural gem. It stayed largely because the Rennert owners threatened a lawsuit if their garage was condemned. The garage was torn down in 1995.

[9] "A New Heart for Baltimore," 89.

[10] The City Fair was later moved uptown to 33rd Street near Memorial Stadium. It was discontinued in the 1990s when funding became scarce.

[11] *Baltimore Sun*, January 15, 1967.

Chapter Three

[1] Quotes from McKeldin's speech, May 21, 1963, McKeldin Papers, series 1, box 11B, McKeldin Library, University of Maryland at College Park.

[2] Wallace, "An Insider's Story of the Inner Harbor," *Planning* (September 1979): 24.

[3] November 3, 1966.

[4] Quoted in John C. Schmidt, "Inner Harbor Progress Report," *Baltimore* (July 1966): 35.

[5] When Miller died in 1972, Walter Sondheim succeeded him as chairman. Millspaugh became president and chief executive officer, and Albert M. Copp became executive vice president and chief operating officer.

[6] *Baltimore Sun*, March 14, 1966.

[7] Script for WBJ-TV editorial (October 9, 1967), series 5, box 40, GBC Collection.

[8] *Baltimore Sun*, November 30, 1979.

[9] Gurney Brekenfield, "Rouse Goes National," *Fortune* (July 27, 1981), 54.

[10] Author interview with Walter Sondheim, February 14, 1994.

Epilogue

[1] *Baltimore Sun*, December 9, 1997.

[2] There are three pedestrian bridges over Pratt Street in the area of the Inner Harbor, but only one, near the National Aquarium, provides access at the street level. It is underused for many of the same reasons that pedestrians shunned the Charles Center walkways. The numerous steps up to the overpass are particularly discouraging.

A Guide to Further Reading

For Baltimore before urban renewal, see Marion E. Warren and Mame Warren, *Baltimore: When She Was What She Used to Be* (Baltimore: Johns Hopkins University Press, 1983); Carleton Jones, *Lost Baltimore Landmarks* (Baltimore: Johns Hopkins University Press, 1993); Jacques Kelly, *Bygone Baltimore: A Historical Portrait* (Norfolk: Donning Co., 1982); Gilbert Sandler, *Jewish Baltimore: A Family Album* (Baltimore: Johns Hopkins University Press, 2000); and Michael R. Farrell, *The History of Baltimore's Streetcars* (Sykesville, Md.: Greenberg Publishing Co., 1992). Christine Rosen discusses the rebuilding of downtown after the fire of 1904 in *The Limits of Power: Great Fires and the Process of City Growth in America* (New York: Cambridge University Press, 1986).

For the urban renewal that started in the 1950s, see Katharine Lyall, "A Bicycle Built for Two: Public-Private Partnership in Baltimore," *National Civic Review,* 72 (1983): 531–71; Marc V. Levine, "Downtown Redevelopment as an Urban Growth Strategy: A Critical Appraisal of the Baltimore Renaissance," *Journal of Urban Affairs,* 9 (1987): 103–23; and David Harvey, "A View from Federal Hill," in Elizabeth Fee, Linda Shopes, and Linda Zeidman, eds., *The Baltimore Book: New Views of Local History* (Philadelphia: Temple University Press, 1991), 227–49; and Michael P. McCarthy, "Renaissance Rivalry in Baltimore: One Charles Center vs. One North Charles," *Maryland Historical Magazine,* 90 (1995): 195–215. W. Edward Orser, *Blockbusting in Baltimore: The Edmondson Village Story* (Lexington: University of Kentucky Press, 1994) discusses the racial aspects of the urban renewal years.

A good introduction to the origins of Charles Center from the perspective of participants is Martin Millspaugh, ed., *Baltimore's Charles Center: A Case Study of Downtown Renewal* (Washington, D.C.: Urban Land Institute, 1964). Also Archibald C. Rogers, "Charles Center, Baltimore," *AIA Journal* (March 1959): 30–40. For the Inner Harbor planning, see David A. Wallace, "An Insider's Story of the Inner Harbor," *Planning* (September 1979): 20–24. Other useful articles on the Inner Harbor include Gurney Breckenfeld, "The Rouse Show Goes National," *Fortune* (July 27, 1981): 48–55; "Roundtable on Rouse" in *Progressive Architecture,* 62 (1981): 100–106; "A MXD Takes Off: Baltimore's Inner Harbor," *Urban Land,* 41 (1982): 10–19.

Downtown festival malls are discussed in Bernard J. Frieden and Lynne B. Sagalyn, *Downtown, Inc.: How America Rebuilds Cities* (Cambridge: M.I.T. Press, 1989); and Michael Sorkin, ed. *Variations on a Theme Park: The New American City and the End of Public Space* (New York: Hill and Wang, 1992). For more recent developments in the Inner Harbor, see Peter Richmond, *Ballpark* (New York: Simon & Schuster, 1993); Jon Morgan and Doug Kapustin, *Gaining a Yard: The Building of Baltimore's Football Stadium* (Baltimore: *Baltimore Sun,* 1998); and John Dorsey and James D. Dilts, *A Guide to Baltimore Architecture,* 3rd ed. (Centreville Md.: Tidewater Publishers, 1997), which is a useful architectural survey of Baltimore buildings old and new. See also James D. Dilts and Catherine F. Black, eds., *Baltimore's Cast-Iron Buildings and Architectural Ironwork* (Centreville, Md.: Tidewater Publishers, 1991).

For the expressway debate, see Douglas H. Haeuber, *The Baltimore Expressway Controversy: A Study in the Decision-Making Process* (Baltimore: Johns Hopkins University Center for Metropolitan Planning and Research, 1974); James Bailey, "How S.O.M. Took on the Baltimore Road Gang," *Architectural Forum,* 130 (1969): 40–45; and Michael P. McCarthy, "Baltimore's Highway Wars Revisited," *Maryland Historical Magazine,* 93 (1998): 137–57. Tom Lewis provides an excellent account of the changes the automobile wrought in America in *Divided Highways: Building the Interstate Highways, Transforming American Life* (New York: Viking, 1997). David Rusk discusses the impact of suburban growth as well as strategies for regional cooperation in *Balti-*

more Unbound (Baltimore: The Abell Foundation, 1996).

Useful general references on downtown urban renewal in other cities include Alexander Garvin, *The American City: What Works, What Doesn't* (New York: McGraw-Hill, 1996). Mark I. Gelfand, *A Nation of Cities: The Federal Government and Urban America, 1933–1965* (New York: Oxford University Press, 1975); James Q. Wilson, ed., *Urban Renewal: The Record and the Controversy* (Cambridge: M.I.T. Press, 1965); also Jon C. Teaford, *The Rough Road to Renaissance: Urban Revitalization in America, 1940–1985* (Baltimore: Johns Hopkins University Press, 1990); Carl Abbott, "Five Downtown Strategies: Policy Discourse and Downtown Planning Since 1945," *Journal of Policy History,* 5 (1993): 5–27. Also Joel Schwartz, *The New York Approach: Robert Moses, Urban Liberals and Redevelopment of the Inner City* (Columbus: Ohio State Press, 1993); Carol Herselle Krinksy, *Rockefeller Center* (New York: Oxford University Press, 1978); Thomas H. O'Connor, *Building a New Boston: Politics and Urban Renewal 1950 to 1970* (Boston: Northeastern University Press, 1993); and Michael P. Weber, *Don't Call Me Boss: David Lawrence, Pittsburgh's Renaissance Mayor* (Pittsburgh: University of Pittsburgh Press, 1988).

For the city as a historical artifact, see Larry R. Ford, *Cities and Buildings* (Baltimore: Johns Hopkins University Press, 1994); Paul Groth and Todd W. Bressi, eds., *Understanding Ordinary Landscapes* (New Haven: Yale University Press, 1997); and Kevin Lynch, *The Image of the City* (Boston: M.I.T Press, 1960).

Index